PCP APPROACH
to Money

Finding the Courage You Need
to Control Your Own Retirement

PCP APPROACH
To Money

Finding the Courage You Need
to Control Your Own Retirement

By Sam Foreman

Dedication

I would like to dedicate this book to my wife of 43 years, Kathie, who is the light of my life and the most supportive friend I have ever known. We married when I was 20 and she was 17. "Feel the fear and do it anyway" is a little inside wisdom between Kathie and me, which we came up with during the very early days of our marriage. Like many other couples growing up together, we have faced situations that required personal courage to see them through. Most of these "bumps in the road" were of my own making. When I acknowledge that fact openly, Kathie doesn't correct me, so it must be so. But she has been right by my side all the way, no matter what the trial. And for that I love her even more.

"Feel the fear and do it anyway" is what we used to say to each other when the future was uncertain. It was a challenge to each other, mutually given and mutually accepted, to face the thing head-on and move forward with our lives despite the trepidation we felt.

Table of Contents

Preface

I knew a man once who refused to travel by air. The very thought of boarding a plane and strapping himself into the seat of a jet airliner literally made him shiver. "I can't explain it," he said. "I know it is irrational, but I'm just scared to death of flying."

Our fears and phobias are often irrational, but that doesn't make them any less real. Fear is a fact, even if it is based on delusion. My recommendation to this man was to just spend the day at a busy airport, watching the planes take off and land. Observe the parade of passengers getting on and off the planes. Note the fact that they did so without incident. That should provide the assurance that travel by air is relatively safe.

I don't know if he ever did that. But even if he did, I doubt that such an exercise would convince him that it is safer to fly than it is to drive — a fact that can be proven by statistics. Then again, statistics do not seem to override superstition when it comes to our phobias.

If my friend could have mustered up the courage to fly just one time, however, he would probably have conquered his fear of flying. As far as I know, he still drives or takes a train everywhere he goes. Psychologists say that the key to the *cause* of a certain fear or phobia is the same as the key to *conquering* it: control. When we analyze what gave birth to an irrational fear, it's usually the momentary — and mortifying — loss of control we experienced. In the case of my non-flying friend, he was afraid to turn over his well-being to a pilot and copilot, some overworked air traffic controllers and some mechanics he had never met. I can understand that. Some folks surrender control more quickly than others.

Have you ever had situations where you trusted and had that trust betrayed? I think we all have. Experts say the way to conquer an irrational fear is to plow through it and regain control (perceived or otherwise) by restoring our confidence that all will be OK if we just move forward and take that first step.

A great example of this is found in the Bible. At Joshua 3:7-17, we find Joshua taking over the leadership of more than 2 million Israelites after the death of Moses. The task was to lead them across the Jordan River, into the "promised land." God didn't tell Joshua that he would part the waters of the Jordan. He just told him to go. It was definitely a "feel the fear" moment for Joshua. God also told him to command the priests to go to the edge of the water, step in and stand still. This was the time of year when the Jordan would have been at flood stage. It was definitely a "feel the fear" moment for the priests who were taking that step, too. But they did it anyway.

Feeling the Fear

When Kathie and I used to say to each other, "Feel the fear and do it anyway," it was our way of saying to each other: "This is part of life — challenges around every corner. Don't escape it, learn to embrace it and turn the negative energy into a positive force. Turn the problem into an opportunity to emerge better on the other side of its solution. This is all just part of the adventure, sweetheart. No one promised you a bed of roses. There is no free lunch, no easy ride, no 'A' for effort. Get up in the face of whatever makes you afraid and make it your middle name and have it for lunch. Take its best punch and then get up and say to it, 'Is that all you've got?'"

I was afraid to enter college. "Sam, don't go to college," my high school guidance counselor told me when I was a senior. "Find a vocation and stick with it; you are just not college material." I definitely felt the fear. This advice came from a *guidance counselor!* But, in the end, I decided to do it anyway. In some ways, the guidance counselor was right. I was not your typical student. I found that I excelled at what I wanted to learn but was dismissive of what I considered a waste of time.

As I mentioned, I met Kathie in the middle of my second year, when she was 17 and I was 20. Within six months, we were married. Now I had a reason to apply myself to every course required to obtain my degree, and I did. I even ended up on the Dean's List. Unfortunately, six months later I became very ill and couldn't work or go to school. I never did find out what the illness was, but it lasted several months and reduced my 160-pound frame to 128 pounds. We leaned on each other for support both financially and physically. We both felt the fear …and proceeded with our challenging but happy life.

It was during this time that Kathie secured part-time employment at a drug store in downtown Toledo, making $1.45 per hour. While I was recovering from my illness and somehow finishing the semester, we leaned on each other for support, both financially, psychologically and spiritually. We survived on tomato soup and eggs and the occasional tuna casserole I made for her while she was at work. Our tiny apartment was $33 per month — *utilities included!* It was the early 1970s and the country was in a deep recession, but I finally found a job at a local hospital as a janitor. I worked very hard at my job in an effort to impress my supervisor, the head of housekeeping for the hospital. After a few months, I asked him if the hospital could hire my wife as well. Although it was against the hospital's hiring policy, they made an exception because of my job performance. We quickly became known as the "cleaning couple." Every once in a while, when we were lucky enough to be assigned to the same floor, I would whisk her away to a corner to steal a kiss.

One day we were looking at the job board, and I saw a job posted requiring 2.5 years in college for a new field called, at that time, "inhalation therapy." I had exactly 2.5 years of college. We quickly finished our food and went to the hospital chapel to pray about the opportunity. While we were on our knees, holding hands and praying with our eyes closed, I felt a sharp tug on my collar. It was the chaplain! The next thing I knew, he was

3

escorting us out, giving us a short lecture about "messing around in the house of God." Looking back, I suppose we did look suspect — Kathie in a pink housekeeping dress and I in a khaki uniform, both us very young.

The next day, I applied for and got the job. The administrator of the department was also responsible for the same department at another hospital. He told me he was very impressed because he had seen me working and offered me the job there or at the smaller hospital. I chose the smaller hospital for two reasons: I would be one of four employees at the smaller hospital versus 36 in the larger one. I also thought that it would be better to work around new people who wouldn't view me as "the young janitor." We had faced the fear, felt the thunder of its awful roar and gone ahead anyway. Although this little "rough patch" would not be the last, we had emerged from the challenge stronger for it and determined to see our education through.

Controlling Your Financial Fears

On our journey through life, it can be a fearful proposition to round that corner that separates the workaday world of regular paychecks and a steady job from the unfamiliar territory of retirement. How will I make ends meet when I turn in my notice at work and those regular weekly paychecks stop coming? What if I don't have enough money to pay my bills? What if I have enough at first and then I run out of it? Will I make it through my older years? What will happen to me if I lose my independence? Will I be able to control my own life as I get older? Inflation has been pretty tame for the last few years, but what if it roars back like it did in the 1980s? What's going to happen to Social Security? How will changes in the system affect me? What will happen to me if I get sick? What if I need long-term care?

The "what-ifs" of retirement are the root cause of much of the fear and concern on the part of millions of Americans today. In this book, we will address many of those fears. The question as to how you will make ends meet when you stop receiving a regular paycheck is a big one. Even if you have adequate resources now, we live in a crazy world where unpredictability is the norm. I saw a bumper sticker the other day that said volumes on this subject in just two words: "Life Happens." When life happens to us, and we encounter a bump in the road we weren't expecting, will we have the financial resources to take it in stride? Years ago, retirement used to be compared to a three-legged stool, financially speaking. One leg was your pension; the other two legs were Social Security and your savings, respectively.

Pensions have almost vanished from the American workplace. This was an account your employer provided for you. Once you retired, your pension was paid for the rest of your life. Defined *benefit* pension plans have been replaced by defined *contribution* retirement plans, such as the 401(k) or 403(b). With these arrangements, you are responsible for providing your own pension. Your employer may match your contributions, if you are lucky. The only problem is (a) those plans are typically not immune from the volatility of the stock market and (b) you can run out of money. So how do you know that you have saved enough? Is this a source of anxiety among seniors? You bet it is.

When Jackson National Life and the Center for Financial Insight surveyed 500 people between the ages of 45 and 65, they found that the younger group — those within 20 years of retirement — listed as their greatest retirement concern whether they were saving enough for retirement. Long-term care expenses and other health care concerns finished a distant second and third, respectively.

So how much is enough? One of my favorite TV commercials is the one put out by ING Insurance Company. It's the one where one man is strolling down a neighborhood street, carrying under his arm a large orange number. There is a dollar sign in front of the number and it appears to be over a million dollars. You can't see what the number is exactly because his arm obscures one of the digits. He encounters a neighbor, on a ladder, trimming a hedge. On the top of the hedge rests the word "Gazillion," also starting with a dollar sign.

In their brief conversation you pick up on the fact that the man with the specific number under his arm has done some planning for retirement and is well prepared, while the hedge trimmer has no clue what it will take for him to successfully retire.

The answer to "How much is enough?" is always different. Each individual circumstance is different. What is enough for one person will not be enough for another.

The Jackson Life survey polled people with at least $200,000 available to invest. Some may say, "Two hundred grand? Really?" as if to say, "That's a lot of money," while others may say, "Two hundred grand? Really?" as if to say, "Is that all?" What is that old maxim? "Different strokes for different folks"? It certainly applies to retirement income planning. No two individuals are exactly alike (even identical twins have different fingerprints). No two retirement income plans should be alike. How much you need to have tucked away in savings before you can safely retire is dependent on your goals, values and unique circumstances.

"Feel the fear" also means don't be overconfident when approaching retirement. Although I didn't stay in the medical profession, I learned a great deal about human anatomy while there. When we feel pain, it's our nerves doing their job. They are telling the brain that something is wrong and needs to be attended to right away. When faced with a threat to their financial security, some humans behave like the ostrich: they put their heads in the sand and pretend the threat isn't there.

If you are a baby boomer like me, you probably remember Alfred E. Neuman, the gap-toothed cover boy for Mad Magazine and his motto: "What? Me Worry?" His goofy image is the quintessence of nonchalance. The attitude that some adults display remind me of that boy. What? Me worry about something that is 20 or 30 years down the road? And the nearer retirement looms, the more obvious the challenges that accompany this new phase of our economic lives become, the more incumbent it should be on responsible people to take stock and plan for them.

By "feel the fear," I am not suggesting that we become fretful and morose about the future. Not at all! But it is one thing to be optimistic about what lies around that bend where retirement awaits, and it is quite another to be blithely unaware of the challenges there, pretending they don't exist.

One theme that you will see repeated often in this book is knowing where you are and where you are going financially. I call it understanding the *what, why* and *how long.* When it comes to money, overconfidence — which is the worst tripping hazard out there because it is unnoticeable — is borne from a lack of education. There is a sliding scale of overconfidence. The more we don't know, the more overconfident we become.

The most overconfident of all are the ones who don't know that they don't know. They can't learn because they don't think they need to. They are also the ones who, when they learn that their retirement portfolio has been sawn apart by the buzz saw of market risk, say the loudest, "What happened?" When the stock market is soaring and each day sees a new high, many of those investors have the face of Alfred E. Neuman, the famed *Mad Magazine* poster boy for insouciance — no worries here! They forget just how quickly their retirement accounts were siphoned during the 2008-2009 bear market, when stocks lost more than half their value in just over a year.

"Feel the fear and do it anyway" put another way is: "Understand the challenges that accompany retirement and take action to meet them." I love the quote by American inspirational writer Orison Swett Marden, who gave us such works as "He Can Who Thinks He Can," and "The Joys of Living." It goes like this: "Obstacles are like wild animals. They are cowards but they will bluff you if they can. If they see you are afraid of them… they are liable to spring upon you; but if you look them squarely in the eye, they will slink out of sight."

Throughout this book, I intend to look some of the obstacles to a worry-free retirement squarely in the eye, much as a primary care physician wouldn't hesitate to point out the areas of your health that may be in jeopardy. Spoiler alert: You may encounter some ideas that are new to you. I can't apologize for that. As a conscientious financial advisor, I am responsible for my advice. Therefore, I am interested in what **works,** not in what ***doesn't.*** If you are one who panics at the mere thought of an unconventional approach, then this book is not for you. Thanks for reading this far, and contact me or one of the members of my staff listed at the end of this book, and we will refund the purchase price to you.

But if you would like to have myths exposed and truth explored, then read on. If you are tired of all the advice you get from those who are pushing a political agenda or trying to sell you a financial product, then stay tuned.

Some of the modern strategies and solutions that characterize financial planning for the 21st century may be unfamiliar to you. Don't let that throw you. Keep an open mind, please. One of the phobias that we have as we grow older is fear of change. It would be a pleasant and cozy world if the world around us remained static when it comes to investing and managing our money, but that is not the way it is in real life.

We are afloat on a river that is constantly in motion. We can either take the wheel and navigate those waters or find ourselves awash in them. There will be rapids. This is where the water moves swiftly over obstacles that lie beneath. Don't blanch at them. This is life in motion. Grip the wheel. Feel the fear and do it anyway.

CHAPTER ONE

Conquering Fear of the Future

"Many of our fears are tissue-paper-thin, and a single courageous step would carry us clear through them."
– Brendan Francis

Unfortunately, I have known too many people who seem to suffer from what I call the "getting ready to get ready" syndrome. They want everything to be just perfect before they start something. They check with all their friends first. "Should I do this? Should I do that?" They never seem to get around to actually doing anything.

"Lord, what is it you want me to do?" they may ask piously. But if waiting for God's voice is a cover for laziness or indecision, they would do better to get out of "it's-all-about-me" mode and take that step. It's not all about you, it's all about *Him.* As did those ancient priests, take the step first and let him part the waters and direct your path.

When it comes to retirement, the primary fear among older Americans is outliving their resources.

I remember reading that statement a few years ago, but at the time, I wondered about its veracity. If I were guessing the greatest fear, I would have listed the Grim Reaper, or perhaps a debilitating illness, such as cancer or Alzheimer's. But a poll conducted in May 2010 by the Allianz Life Insurance Company of North America revealed that 61 percent of Americans between the ages of 44 and 75 listed their greatest fear as living longer than their financial resources could carry them. That fear outranked death, disease, snakes, spiders, tornados, earthquakes, floods or having your credit card stolen. But when you stop and think about it, that fear is understandable. It's not about the money. Not really. No one wants to die, but I have it on good authority that everyone eventually will. The fate worst feared is losing your independence and becoming a burden those you love.

According to a 2011 study conducted by the Society of Actuaries, in the United States most people underestimate how long they will live. Of course, life expectancy is impossible to predict on an individual level, but there are some interesting statistics that have come out lately about longevity. The SOA calculates that the *average* life expectancy for an American male is 85 and for a female, 88. A 65-year-old male has about a one in four chance of living to age 92. Females who reach age 65 have a one in four chance of living to age 94.

The way life expectancy tables are calculated, the longer you live, the longer you will probably life. In other words, if you make it to age 70, odds are more favorable that you will live to age 90.

What drops out the bottom is this: Most people under-plan for retirement because they can't see themselves being in it as long as they probably will be. In 1960, when most TVs were black and white and cars still had tail fins, the average life expectancy for American males was 66.6 years. It has inched up almost two years each decade since then. Not even the experts know why. Some credit advancements in medicine and others say it's because we are taking better care of ourselves. Regardless of the reason, from a retirement income planning perspective, it's part of the equation.

The Allianz pollsters asked 3,247 people how much annual income they would need in retirement. The average response was $59,000 per year. The follow up question was, "How much will you have to save to create that kind of income?" Most people said, "I don't know." Those who ventured a guess were way short.

10

The Baby Boomer Retirement Stampede

That sound you hear like distant thunder is the stampede of baby boomers headed for retirement. To be an official baby boomer you must have to have been born between 1946 and 1964. That means that the first batch of baby boomers started turning 65 in 2011, and by some estimates they are retiring at the rate of 10,000 per week. Imagine that! Ten thousand people per week signing up for Medicare and collecting their Social Security and contemplating retirement!

Baby boomers are called that because of the sharp spike in the birth rate that occurred after World War II. When the war ended, the returning soldiers and sailors settled down to family life. Statisticians sometimes refer to the boom generation as the "pig in the python," referring to the bulge in the birthrate that started after the war, peaked in the 1950s and began tapering off by the 1960s. This generation would affect the world more than any other generation previously. Baby boomers invented Velcro and rock and roll. They grew up watching black-and-white TV, learned to live with the shadow of nuclear war and saw with their own eyes the miracle of men placing footprints on the moon.

Birthdates aside, you may be a baby boomer if you know the following:

- The first names of the Everly Brothers and what time Susie had to be home.

- The names of all four of the Beatles.

- What makes Popeye strong to the finish?

- Where do M&Ms melt?

- What was Brylcreem used for?

- What helps build strong bodies 12 ways?

- What was Gracie's response to "Say good night, Gracie"?

- The answer to "Hey, kids! What time is it?"

- The first names of the two Maverick brothers.

I was born on May 29, 1950, which makes me an official member of the baby boomer generation. Like many other boomers, I can attest to the fact that the milestones of life tend to whiz by very quickly when you're having fun. As one member of the boom generation put it: "One minute we were in our 30s, and we blinked, and now we are our parents' age." While boomers set the record for earning power, as a group they weren't good savers. According to the Employee Benefit Research Institute (EBRI), 56 percent of workers surveyed say they have less than $25,000 in savings. Nearly 30 percent of workers of all ages surveyed aren't confident they'll have enough to retire and 36 percent of workers say they expect to have to keep working after age 65.

Many Americans close to retirement age are not only lacking in savings — some are over their heads, financially speaking. The EBRI survey found that 42 percent of retirees say their current level of debt is a problem.

Many in this current crop of retirees have experienced what economists call the "lost decade." Averaging out the peaks and valleys of the stock market, they have had no growth. Two vicious bear markets have chewed up their 401(k)s and some have been forced to take distributions from investment portfolios that were at a fraction of their peak value. The Great Recession of 2008 was bad timing for those approaching retirement then. Declining property values drained home equity — the little "kitty" that many were counting on to see them through.

Using the numbers put out by traditional financial planners who recommended an exclusively market-based retirement scenario, a 65-year-old retiree requires $1.1 million in savings to draw $50,000 a year when you factor in inflation. That's assuming both a 5 percent annual return on those investments and a 3 percent inflation rate. However, that 5 percent return is unlikely given the stock market performance since 2000.

Making It Better

My wife Kathie and I both came from the medical field. I was a therapist working with both heart and lung patients and in the diagnostics area. My goal working with the patients was to find out exactly what the problem was and then figure out how to make it better. When I entered the financial advisory profession, I decided it just made sense to do the same thing when it comes to retirement plans. When Kathie and I began to come up with a mission statement for Generations Financial Group, we ran through several phrases and expressions, searching for just the right one that summarized what exactly what we were all about professionally. The one we finally landed on was "We Believe in Better." Snap — that was it!

Just as in our former lives helping people with their physical challenges, we were now able to use our skills and education to find better solutions, achieve better results, discover better approaches and come up with better answers to improve our clients' lives. What were they doing now and how could we help them do it better? We would constantly be looking for new ways to tackle problems. One of the first things we decided to do was use more of a teaching approach, starting with the math of investing. For example, consider how most people think when it comes to big losses in their portfolio. We found that most investors are told that if they hold a portfolio of stocks to expect losses from time to time, but if they just hang in there, the market bounces back. And that is essentially true. What they aren't told, however, is how the math works in a market that is in recovery mode. Therefore, most don't realize how important it is, when you are approaching retirement, to avoid big losses in a portfolio. Here's what I mean:

Let's say that you had $100,000 invested in the stock market and then you lost 50 percent, how much do you have to gain to get back even? If you answered 50 percent, you are in the same boat as most people. When I ask that question at public educational seminars on investing, that is the first response I hear. Then I pause and let the silence fill the room. Usually, someone with a math brain will come up with the right answer — 100 percent. If you have $100,000 invested, you subsequently lose 50 percent — reducing your balance to $50,000 — and the market goes back up 50 percent, you would reap only $25,000. You need another 50 percent gain, or 100 percent total gain, to get back to $100,000.

THE POWER OF LOSS

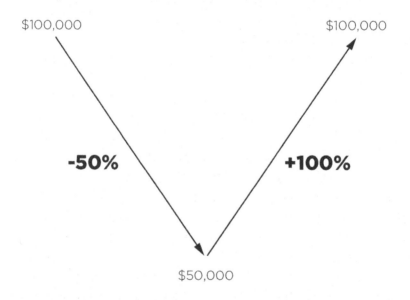

In 2008, the average investor lost about the same as the market, 37 percent. It took a 60 percent gain to come back from that, and for most people it took more than four years. This was problematic for most retirees. Why? Because they didn't have four years to wait. The timing of the crash forced them to unplug themselves from the market and begin making withdrawals. What would have happened, however, if the portfolio had only an 8 percent loss? It only takes 1 percent more (9 percent), to come back to come back from that. When we apply a little math to the equation it is easy to see that in a market that is unpredictable, unstable and volatile, it is crucially important to avoid big losses. Average returns are also overrated. If you have a 50 percent gain, then a 50 percent loss, then a 50 percent gain, then a 50 percent loss, your average return is zero, but your real return at the end of that is a negative 40.79 percent!

What? Why? How Long?

First, if you are in the market, you need to have a **reason**. I remember way back in August of 2000, a major financial magazine recommended buying 10 stocks to retire comfortably. That was almost 14 years ago as of this writing. Had you purchased those stocks and hung onto them, you would still be down more than 40 percent. You must have a *reason* to invest, not just because some magazine says so.

Here are three important questions to consider when investing. You need to know **what, why** and **how long** on all of your investments. I sometimes have people who were referred to me come in for a consultation about their investments. It is quite common for the consultation to go as follows: They show me the portfolio, which usually contains mutual funds. I will pick one of them out and begin asking questions.

"Mr. and Mrs. Jones, I see you have here several thousand dollars in this growth and income fund. Can you explain to me *what* this fund is?"

They may struggle a bit for an answer, but eventually they will say, "**We don't know.**"

"Tell me, do you know *who* is running this fund?"

"We don't know that either."

"How long have they been there?"

"We don't know."

"What is the rating on the fund?"

"We don't know."

"Can you name just three companies in this fund?"

"We don't know."

"I am sure you are aware that in 2008, it was the financial companies that played a large part in bringing the market down. What percent of your money in this fund is invested in the financials?"

"We don't know."

"Let's move on to another question…***Why*** do you have this fund?"

"We don't know."

"How long do you plan on keeping this fund?"

"We don't know."

I don't do this to embarrass or insult anyone. I do it to bring home the point that you simply must know the answers to the ***what, why*** and ***how long*** when it comes to investing. Anything other than that is just a **"hope"** strategy — hoping it works out. Yes, you probably could have gotten away with that in the 1990s, when the market knew only one direction — up. In those heady days, you could take the stock market page from the newspaper, tack it to the wall, throw a dart at it, invest in the stock represented by the ticker symbol penetrated by the point of the dart, and come out smelling like a rose. But things are moving much faster now. The market is easily spooked by international threats, currency problems, a rise in the federal deficit numbers, ad infinitum. This makes it even more imperative that you invest with your eyes open. It is crucial that you know the ***reason*** for your investment choices.

Safe Investing Eliminates Fear

Generations Financial Group's client appreciation dinners are memorable events. In 2012, we filled the Pinnacle banquet hall in Maumee, Ohio, with 780 guests who enjoyed the food, fellowship and fun. We hired a professional magician and there was the standard fare of music and dancing. I was even pressed into service to do impersonations of Dean Martin, Elvis Presley and Louis Armstrong. But what I appreciated most about the evening was the opportunity to meet and talk with clients in an informal atmosphere where we could get to know each other as people.

More than once, individuals with whom I had worked to develop a "better solution" approached me and sincerely thanked me because, when others were getting hammered in the market during the 2008-2009 Wall Street sell-off, their life savings remained intact. While some of their friends were experiencing sleepless nights over market losses, they were able to sleep at night in the secure knowledge that they were protected by the safe-money investment strategies they chose to put in place. I was again reminded of why I chose to become a financial advisor and how important this mission was to always be "making it better" for these wonderful people.

CHAPTER TWO

Finding the Courage to Forge Ahead

"Inaction breeds doubt and fear. Action breeds confidence and courage. If you want to conquer fear, do not sit home and think about it. Go out and get busy."
– Dale Carnegie

I didn't find my "calling" until in the middle years of my life. In other words, I had a lot of *occupations* and held down many *jobs*...but I didn't find my professional passion until later on.

As soon as I was old enough to fetch and carry, I worked on the family farm, milking cows and feeding chickens. My first actual "paycheck" job was working as a porter at a plaza on the Ohio Turnpike at the tender age of 14. When I graduated high school at age 18, the turnpike people gave me my own plaza to manage.

My father, K. Doyle Foreman, was well known as a hard-working man. He worked at the Autolite factory in Toledo, Ohio, running a punch press, which he considered his "day job." His other job was tending the 80-acre farm. Dad died at 62 of a heart attack, but he instilled in us six boys the principles of industry and seeing a job through to its finish. We were referred to as "the hard-working Foreman boys" around the little town of Berkey, Ohio, where I grew up. My mother, a really hard worker and always the encourager, took care of the house and gardens, along with my sister. Mom died at age 98.

I told you earlier that one of the reasons I love my wife so much is that she always believed in me and knew that I would eventually find what I was put on earth to do. And that's not all. Our journey together had more than its share of disappointments and travail. She remained by my side through the disappointments as well as the joy.

As a kid, I wanted to sample all the flavors of ice cream before I decided what flavor I liked the best. I also found myself intrigued by any task, sometimes even the menial ones. Cleaning out the chicken coop? I would be the best chicken coop cleaner there ever was! I don't regret having sampled the flavor of several vocations before I found what I really wanted to do. All the personal evaluation tests I took indicated that I was good at math and loved and enjoyed people. I loved solving problems. I was cut out to be a "people's number-problem solver." But what did that mean? All of that became crystal clear when I found myself in a position to help people pick up the pieces of their financial lives after the market crash of 2000. But please let me explain what led up to that.

Finding the Right Place to Be

When I first started college, I had no idea what to major in. I picked, of all things, theatre. After all, I did land the lead in a high school play. Was that my calling — to be a professional actor? I did fall quickly in love with all the courses. It was fun and it taught me communication skills that I treasure to this day. But it was fun, not education. When I applied for and got the job as a respiratory therapist (a job I needed to pay for my education), I suddenly found myself in a science atmosphere. It didn't take me long to figure out that I needed to take courses in chemistry and physics. Respiratory therapy involves complex equipment. I would also need to complete a cardio-pulmonary technology course and obtain credentials in diagnostics. I was on a fast track. Eighteen months into my new job, I was running the Respiratory Therapy department, which included a much-needed raise in pay. My earnings were paying for Kathie's first year of nursing school. When she got a job as a nurse, her earnings would pay for my further education in respiratory therapy.

The hospital doubled in size, my patient load grew larger, and so did the size of my family. My increased salary enabled Kathie to press the pause button on her nursing career and care for the children. I didn't know it at the time, but I would soon be solving clients' financial problems instead of solving patients' heart and lung problems. Before that was to occur, however, my career path took an unexpected turn.

One of the top administrators of the hospital suggested that I should get my master's degree in business and become a hospital administrator. With a smile, I thought about the guidance counselor who told me not to go to pursue higher education. For someone who "wasn't cut out for college," I was sure racking up an interesting assortment of degrees. Many times I wondered how God was going to use this mixed-up mess of education I had acquired.

The kids got older and Kathie continued her training, eventually becoming a Registered Nurse. I added an MBA to my three other degrees and became a hospital administrator. I should have been a happy camper. But the further I got from patient care, the unhappier I became.

Entering the Financial Profession

The idea of becoming a financial professional never occurred to me until, one day, I had lunch with a friend who was a professional engineer and a licensed financial professional. I had become disillusioned with the politics and bureaucracy of the corporate world. But to become licensed in insurance and securities would require — you guessed it — *more education!*

Sometimes events occur that make your decisions for you. When I had endured about as much of the politics and bureaucracy of hospital administration as I could stand, I realized

I needed to change direction. I felt the old familiar fear again. Was I sure? Change becomes less attractive the older we get. But, with Kathie's prodding, encouragement and support, I turned in my notice to leave the corporate world and strode forth to begin building my own financial advisory practice. I took a position with a major brokerage and soon moved into management. I found my niche building branch offices — first my own and then seven more in neighboring towns. I studied for and eventually obtained nearly all the licenses one could obtain in the financial profession. I had Series 7, Series 63 and Series 24 licenses, and I had founded my own Registered Investment Advisor firm.

Another Feel the Fear Moment

One of my favorite quotes of all time is by Theodore Roosevelt, a man whose personal courage made him legendary: "Far better is it to dare mighty things, to win glorious triumphs, even though checkered by failure, than to take rank with those poor spires who neither enjoy much nor suffer much because they live in the gray twilight that knows not victory or defeat."

By the mid-1990s I had enjoyed some glorious triumphs. The seven branch offices I had worked hard to establish were doing well. I had developed an investing model using noncorrelative styles and my client's accounts were producing good results. All was, as they say, smooth sailing and full speed ahead. But I was about to encounter some of the "checkered by failure" about which Mr. Roosevelt so eloquently spoke in the form of a man we shall call Ron, who came to help us with our computer system.

Computers were just becoming an indispensable part of business in 1996. There were programs and applications that required technical know-how that we simply didn't possess. Ron had come to us highly recommended as someone who not only knew computers, but who also had a working knowledge of the investment business, having once been licensed in securities. He was a friendly guy, and seemed quite sincere in his desire to help us. Oddly, Ron would take no pay for his services.

As time passed, we began receiving strange faxes from Ron about commodity pools. Commodity pools are similar to mutual funds in that the investors' assets are pooled in order to make trades that would not be possible for each individual investor. Many hedge funds are commodity pools. But the financial world is heavily regulated. Banks are regulated by the Federal Reserve Board. Stock brokers are regulated by the Securities and Exchange Commission (SEC) and Financial Industry Regulatory Authority (FINRA.)

Commodity pools fall under a different regulatory agency, known as the Commodity Futures Trading Commission (CFTC). So it was one of those things I knew we weren't set up for. But Ron said these were different. These were *"friends and family* commodity pools" and couldn't we at least meet with a specialist he knew who could fill us in on the details? If we did, we would find out in quick order that this type of investing would "pass the test" with the SEC.

Ron's friend, the specialist, was knowledgeable. The setting for our meeting was quite impressive — his 11,000-square-foot home. In his office was a bank of computers with which he tracked all the markets simultaneously. I reiterated to the specialist, whom we shall call Jack, my belief that this was outside the area of finance for which we were licensed and would put us out of compliance with SEC rules. Jack not only insisted that I was wrong, but was able to quote certain sections of the code that indicated there would be no problem with "friends and family" commodity pools.

"Call the compliance officer at your broker-dealer home office and ask," Jack said persuasively. "See if they don't give you a pass on 'friends and family' pools."

I did call. And I was surprised to hear the answer that, no, they were not concerned about "friends and family" pools. I was told that we would not even have to list it as an outside business activity. Even so, I wasn't sure it was a direction we wanted to go. We were doing well and our plates were pretty full. I discussed it with other managers in the main branch and we unanimously decided that, even though we were informed that it would be no violation of the rules, we would still decline. We just didn't see how we would be able to fit it in.

I met with Ron the next day to give him our decision and the reasons behind it. In hindsight, if there is one take-away from these events, it is this: Whenever someone says "no problem," look for the problem.

"No problem," Ron said, "I will personally oversee the program. Don't worry about a thing." You have to remember: This is the man who had solved our technical problems and, over seven months, gained our trust. Once again, he was going above and beyond just to help us. Regretfully, we let him.

Later in 1996, several family members of individuals at our firm began to participate in the program, as did we ourselves, all in the name of the partnership Ron had conveniently set up for us. At first, nothing was noticeably wrong. Then in early 1997, things turned sour. Ron, our charismatic helper, suddenly disappeared. He just didn't show up at the office one day. One of his associates, who was also duped, helped us figure out what Ron had been doing. Ron and Jack had been falsifying reports to us. The reality was that they had bilked our friends and our family for an enormous sum of money. We immediately reported our findings to the compliance department of the broker-dealer. They assured me that there was "no problem" and that they would fly someone out from the compliance department the next day.

When the broker-dealer's compliance officer arrived she again assured me that there was nothing to worry about. She went through Ron's files, took copies of everything, and left. The next day the broker-dealer called to tell me I was fired. Next, we received a call from the FBI asking questions about Ron. Ron would eventually turn himself over to the authorities, saying he felt guilty for what he had done to us, but the money was gone like so much smoke in the wind.

24

Ron had been working with 25 accounts, all under our name, containing $1.2 million. Talk about "feeling the fear": This was heart-stopping and bone-chilling. My entire life had been built around helping people and now, to my horror, I discovered that not only had I failed to help them, I had inadvertently hurt them. Making matters worse was the fact that most of these people were either close friends or members of my own family. I had never been so low. I saw all that Kathie and I had worked so hard for evaporating before my eyes. How could trusting one man lead to all of this? At this point I didn't want to live.

Just as those who survive a horrible car accident will sometimes sit and replay the events leading up to the crash over and over, I began to replay these events over and over in my mind. My involvement in this debacle was not the result of an impulsive decision. The relationship that Ron had built with us was carefully orchestrated over seven months. All of his assertions as to the legitimacy of the operation were supported by reams of documentation. The man had come to us highly recommended. I even knew his father, who was a surgeon at one of the hospitals where I had served as an administrator. The money was gone. The branches were gone. I had no broker-dealer. I was still licensed at that point, but I was not allowed to speak to any of my other clients. I believe now that the only thing that kept me going at that time was my relationship with God and my wife's prayers. At one of those low moments, Kathie reached across the table and squeezed my hand. I looked up to see that same wry smile I had come to love when we first met those many summers ago. "Feel the fear," she said. I found myself mouthing the words that completed the sentence. It had become our mutual contract for what to do in the face of adversity. "And do it anyway," I answered.

A New Beginning

I eventually contacted another brokerage house. This organization was smaller and the owners were willing to listen to my side of the story. Fortunately, they had a former NASD (National Association of Securities Dealers, now called FINRA) attorney on their staff who was eager to hear about what had happened to us and why. More than that, he believed us. He was also confident that we would be treated favorably at an NASD hearing. The broker-dealer hired us and within 30 days we were able to reach out to our clients. With the help of attorneys, we developed a plan to repay all of our friends and family members who had lost money.

We invited all those who had lost money to a meeting and explained everything that had happened. They were gracious and understanding beyond our wildest expectations. They unanimously agreed to our repayment plan and none of them seemed to hold us personally responsible for what had happened. However, as soon as the CFTC discovered that we had an accepted arrangement in place to repay those who had lost money, they put a stop to it, insisting that it be handled through the courts instead.

We made several trips to the CFTC in Chicago. They were convinced that we were guilty of intentionally defrauding these people, even though they had received letters from our friends and family stating that they trusted us and knew we would make good on our promise to refund their money. We even had to petition the court before we could give them any of their money back. The investigations and negotiations between our attorneys and the CFTC went on for almost two years. Finally, in mid-1999, we agreed to accept the wording of the CFTC settlement, clearing us to proceed with "their" repayment plan, beginning March of 2000. The wording of the CFTC settlement made us equally and individually responsible for repayment. But it wasn't over yet. We still had the NASD panel to deal with, and the panel's investigation began immediately after the settlement with the CFTC. A negative vote there could put us back out of business.

When we met with the NASD panel, a former NASD attorney who represented our current broker-dealer was in attendance. It looked as if the skies were finally beginning to clear. Our broker-dealer was pulling for us. The panel noted that our records had been perfectly compliant up until Ron had entered the picture as well as after the incident, while working for the new broker-dealer. Everyone who had been hurt by the program wrote a letter to the NASD petitioning them to allow us to keep our licenses. Our new broker-dealer told us that they had received word that the panel was going to recommend to the NASD board that we keep our security licenses. We were further encouraged to hear that the board nearly always approved the recommendation of these panel members. We felt like the nightmare may actually finally be over.

The board, inexplicably, went against the panel's recommendation. We no longer had a license. We were out of business. Although not a permanent bar to holding a license, it was bad enough. So, here we were, with a staff and a large office and the inability to make any income. We still felt responsible to repay those who lost money on our watch. But we had nowhere else to go. The youngest of the three of us just left and moved to another state. We were finished. It was over. Or so it seemed.

Another New Beginning

I am convinced that God designed us so that we have lots of new beginnings. Every day is a new beginning. After a long and tiring day, we close our eyes and go into a state of unconscious for eight hours or so; then we awaken to a golden new day. Each year, the green leaves of summer turn to gold and red, they fall from the trees and all living creatures await the spring — another new beginning. Thank you, Lord. We need those do-overs...some of us more than others.

A week after the NASD death sentence, I received a call from a San Diego firm, asking me to come out and evaluate an annuity marketing program. I was still licensed in this field, but I didn't really know much about annuities. I had been a Registered Investment Advisor and stock broker. But the episode with Ron and company had cost me a fortune and sullied my reputation. With nothing to lose, I left for California and in the winter of 1999, I decided to give it a try.

More than 80 people attended the first public educational seminar I gave in the Toledo, Ohio, area. They were eager to hear what I had to say and, needless to say, I was delighted to be back at work, analyzing and creating plans, solving problems again. Then there was another devastating blow. The local newspaper came out with an article announcing my name and claiming that my Registered Investment Advisor license had been "revoked." If you have ever been castigated and lied about in the press, you know how I felt — helpless and powerless to fight back. It wasn't true! My Registered Investment Advisor license was *withdrawn,* not *revoked.*

The state issued a correction for the misinformation they supplied to the paper, but by that time the damage had been done, and there was no point in having the paper print the correction. One by one, people came back to my office to ask for their files back. It was another dark day. How many more times did I have it in me to feel the fear, and the anguish of failure, and still press ahead?

With a heavy heart, I called the San Diego office of the new firm and told the two leaders of the organization to which I had attached myself that there was no use continuing. There was a few seconds of silence on the other end. Then they both began speaking at once, telling me that I was wrong to call it quits and that I shouldn't give up. I wanted to believe them, so I pressed them for a reason. They said they didn't really know me all that well, but they simply had a good feeling about me. They encouraged me to give it another try.

When you are down on yourself, how reassuring it is for others to believe in you. Slowly but surely, I rebuilt my practice once again. After a year, I was doing OK. My clients loved the work I was doing for them, and it was rewarding to be solving problems again. But I was frustrated, being unable to use all of the training I had received on the securities side. Having been a

28

Registered Investment Advisor for several years, I knew just how to solve many of their problems, but I simply lacked the ability to do anything about it. It was like a singer losing his voice. I had to refer them to someone else because I was only able to work with insurance products.

Kathie saw how frustrated I was. By this time, she had resumed her career and was working as an RN in the emergency room of a local hospital. She came to me one day and said, "I can't stand to see you this way any longer. I am going to go for my securities licenses so we can work together and give your people all the help they need." She gave up her nursing career to link arms with me.

Not long after that conversation, she had all the securities licenses, including the registered Investment Advisor Representative license she needed so that we could create a complete financial plan for people. To protect her license, she had to set up a separate company and create a strategic alliance. Later, we added a tax service. Throughout all of this, I made an amazing discovery. It was one of those epiphanies like inventors have when they accidentally spill one chemical onto another and, in the process, change the world for the better.

Prior to my involvement with annuities, I was one-dimensional when it came to investing and wealth management. Had it not been for the disaster caused by Ron and his "friends and family commodity pools" fiasco, I may have never learned the height, width and depth of annuities and how they can be used in retirement income planning. I was a securities man through and through. Some who come from an insurance background and know all about annuities don't understand the securities business and how it can be used to structure financial plans for growth and income. As a consequence, these two poles of the financial advisory spectrum are often at odds with each other.

Advisors squabble and fight about whose approach is better. I discovered that the truth is in the middle. Depending on the circumstances, both securities and annuities can be used to form the basis of a solid, specialized financial plan. As you continue reading, you will see exactly what I mean. With all of the difficulties we faced and conquered, the lesson Kathie and I learned was simple and crystal clear: God often has a better plan, but sometimes we just get in the way.

What has made us so successful over the past 15 years has been timing — God's timing. Back in late 1999, when I did my first public educational seminar, things fell apart. I tried again in January 2000. Remember, that was when the stock market was going strong. Then a few months later, the market tumbled. The strategies I was able to put together — combining the safety of annuities and the reasonable, non-correlative approach to market investing — preserved the portfolios of many of my clients when history repeated itself with the market crash of 2008. How grateful I am that we didn't quit. How thankful I am that Kathie and I felt that tingle of fear with each setback, reached for each other's hand and went forward to do it anyway.

CHAPTER THREE

Dealing with the Risks of Investing

"Hesitation increases in relation to risk
in equal proportion to age."

– Ernest Hemingway

When tragedies occur, we develop 20/20 hindsight as to what could have prevented them. When examined in the light of history, the collection of "what ifs" and "if onlys" becomes a mosaic of linked possibilities. If only passenger airplanes had secured cockpit doors in 2001, the World Trade Center attacks that took place on 9/11 would never have occurred. If only the missiles fired into a known al Qaeda training camp in 1998 had been launched two hours earlier, Osama bin Laden would have been eliminated three years before 9/11 and nearly 3,000 lives could have been spared. The list is endless.

The sinking of the Titanic on the night of April 14, 1912, was one of the most heartbreaking events in history. Out of the 2,223 passengers aboard the doomed ship, only 706 survived. Now, over 100 years later, the Titanic tragedy still moves and intrigues people. The discovery of the ship's wreckage in 1985 has given historians new information regarding the disaster. In hindsight, there were so many little things that could have prevented the sinking if only the right people had known about them. If only the captain had known that a mammoth iceberg had broken away from the Arctic ice field and drifted far into the shipping lane. If only the two lookouts in the crow's nest had known that the absolutely clear conditions that night would create a mirage horizon that served to camouflage the iceberg. And so on.

Knowing the risks we face in any endeavor can lessen the chance of catastrophe. Let's face it — retirement is an uncharted landscape. I was speaking at a public event shortly after the 2008 market crash when one attendee walked up to me after the program and asked me if I knew what was going to happen next on Wall Street. The news had just come out that the government was going to have to bail out a couple of the nation's largest banks and one of the country's too-big-to-fail automakers. I told him I couldn't predict the future. To lighten the mood, I said that the only crystal ball I had was one of those shake-it-up-and-watch-it-snow paper weights someone had brought me back from a vacation trip, and no matter how hard I shook it, it didn't tell me a thing.

I noticed he tried to give me a weak smile, but the man was deeply upset. I would learn later that he had lost almost $250,000 in the market freefall — a small fortune to most people. This was half of his life's savings and, besides Social Security, represented his only other source of retirement income. I wished I could have given him a better answer. "I feel like I'm in the middle of a minefield and no one seems to have a map to the darned thing," he said.

I gave that a lot of thought as I drove back to my office that day. In many respects, I do have a "map to the minefield," so to speak. This man, if he had an advisor, had been given bad advice. His advisor had, either knowingly or unknowingly, allowed him to walk into dangerous territory. Bad advice is often not malicious; it is, typically, merely the absence of good advice.

In the financial advisory community, there are those whose education is limited to stock trading. They only speak the language of Wall Street. They can't give clients holistic planning advice because they aren't acquainted with 21st-century strategies of money management or tax and asset preservation. They know nothing about alternative investments and retirement income planning strategies. Their needle is stuck on the same scratch in the record: buy-and-hold, buy-and-hold, buy-and-hold. The more aggressive brokers are even more dangerous with their attempts to time the market and pick hot stocks. No one can time the market — not effectively, anyway. Markets are unpredictable by nature. Our man with the quarter-million-dollar hole in his pocket had been given bad directions and now found himself lost and in trouble.

The remainder of this chapter will focus on some of the risks and hazards investors face today. I am a big believer in the sentiment expressed by what is known as the Serenity Prayer: "God, grant me the serenity to accept the things I cannot change, the courage to change the things I can, and wisdom to know the difference." Just like the iceberg that sank the Titanic, there are a number of risks and hazards we face as we make our way through retirement that we won't be able to change. They are threats, either real and current or potential. They can, however, be sidestepped if we know where they lie — that's the map to the minefield, so to speak.

Inflation Risk

Inflation is defined as an increase in the price of goods and services compounded by a decline in the purchasing power of money. For example, if the annual inflation rate is 3 percent, then a $1 candy bar will cost $1.03 in a year. When I am preparing a financial plan, I usually allow for a 3 percent inflation rate. If a steady inflation rate of 2 to 3 percent — which is what the economy is experiencing at the time of this writing — can be likened to the steady erosion caused by a slow-moving stream, then hyperinflation, which comes along every now and then, is the floodwater that can wash away an entire town.

Inflation is like a monster that, for the moment, is under sedation. But some can remember a time in the late 1970s when someone let the monster out of its cage for a couple of years. President Jimmy Carter was in the White House at the time; people wore polyester and listened to disco. Carter may get the blame for those inflationary times, but the seeds of it were sown when Lyndon B. Johnson was president in the mid-1960s. Johnson's social programs (remember The Great Society) and the Vietnam War had placed a serious drain on the U.S. Treasury, a situation he passed along to his successor, Richard M. Nixon, who was inaugurated on Jan. 20, 1969.

Inflationary pressure began to build in the early 1970s. Nixon imposed wage and price controls in 1971, and they seemed to work for a spell, but inflationary pressure continued to build. Two things happened after that: One, the controls were lifted, which caused a dramatic surge in prices and wages. Two, in order to print more money (which always fuels the fires of inflation), Nixon broke the last link connecting American currency to gold. This led to a devaluation of the American dollar, which was like throwing gasoline on a fire.

When Nixon resigned, a casualty of the Watergate investigation, he left the mess to his lame-duck vice-presidential successor, Gerald Ford, who saw inflation soar from an acceptable 3.6 percent to 12 percent in 1974. You may be a baby boomer if you remember the WIN buttons that the president and some members of Congress sported in those days. Ford declared war on inflation with the famous "Whip Inflation Now" speech he delivered to Congress on Oct. 8, 1974. The buttons were the punchline of jokes, however, as they did little good. Some even turned them upside down and said that NIM was an acronym for "Need Immediate Money," or "Nonstop Inflation Merry-go-round."

By the time Jimmy Carter was elected, inflation was out of control, peaking at 14.76 percent in March 1980. It was a fiscal zoo. People saved money at banks incredulous at the double-digits rates on CDs and money market accounts, only to be hit with doubling and tripling prices for groceries and gasoline. The building boom of the mid-1970s screeched to a halt in 1979 when 30-year mortgages entered into double-digit interest rates. Auto manufacturers laid off thousands of workers when prices and interest rates made the purchase of cars prohibitive. Like rain on a forest fire, the recession of the early 1980s was what finally tamed inflation and put the monster back in the cage.

We have come to expect a 2 to 3 percent inflation rate as a matter of course. Could hyperinflation happen again? Who knows, but I do know this: Failure to plan for inflation is imprudent. Inflation pinches retirees harder because their income is less flexible. For example, let's say you needed to supplement your Social Security by $1,000 per month. How big would your nest egg have to be, earning 7 percent interest, if you lived 20 years in retirement? How about if you lived 30 years in retirement? Now figure in 3 percent inflation. How does that affect the picture? One of the financial planning software programs I use allowed me to plug in those variables and the results were enlightening.

Effect of Inflation on Income Requirements

- If you live 20 years in retirement, you need $129,734 to produce $1,000 per month income with no inflation!

- If you live 20 years in retirement, you need $163,007 to produce $1,000 per month income with 3 percent inflation.

- If you live 30 years in retirement, you need $195,343 to produce $1,000 per month income with 3 percent inflation.

Source: Planner Portal Financial Planning Software

Even tame inflation is stealthy. At only 3 percent per year, it is almost imperceptible but it's there. A gallon of gasoline in 1960 cost 29 cents... and they pumped it for you! The average house cost $11,900 in1960 and now you pay that for a 10-year-old used car.

So what will it be 30 years from now? According to the Society of Actuaries, only 72 percent of pre-retirees, and 55 percent of retirees have calculated the effects of inflation on their retirement plan. Ten years into their retirement, however, they will be spending $13 to buy what $10 buys today. In 20 years, they will be spending $18 to buy what $10 buys today.

So that's the hazard. How can you avoid it? You may not be able to completely avoid inflation, but there are some steps you can take to counter it. For example:

- Delay taking your Social Security to age 70, if possible. Typically, your benefits increase by 8 percent per year.

- Consider purchasing a fixed index annuity with an income rider and an inflation rider. Ask your financial advisor about it and make sure it's suitable for your situation.

- Ask your financial advisor to help you develop an inflation-adjusted budget that will spell out the dollar amounts you will need as the years go by.

When planning for retirement, it is impossible to cover all contingencies, but it is wise to figure 3 percent for inflation.

Currency Risk

Pull out a dollar bill and look at it. What is it worth? If you answer "a dollar," you're right of course — technically speaking, at least. But the world is not a simple place, economically. The value of your currency can be affected by shifts in foreign exchange rates. Currency risk is what arises from the change in price of one currency against another. Currency risk is obvious when investors of companies have assets or business operations across national borders. It is not so easy for ordinary investors.

Here's something most people are unaware of. Currency exchange rates can affect all of the following:

- U.S. corporate earnings

- the stock market

- the nation's economic growth rate

But what you don't know can hurt you. The fact is, currency exchange rates open even ordinary U.S. investors to exposure in their portfolios, as well as the individual stocks found in their portfolios. Their investments don't appear, to them at least, to be attached to foreign economies, but appearances can be deceiving in the global economy in which all markets operate today.

The common misconception is that the foreign exchange market — also known as the "forex" or "FX" market — is primarily where the central banks buy and sell their nation's currency and influence macro-economics. And they are right. But what happens more often — in fact, what happens throughout the workweek — is that corporations and banks trade currencies nonstop. Wealthy investors speculate in the foreign exchange market continuously and have for a long while. In the late 1990s, day traders and individual investors gained access to FX trading platforms that were formerly the sole dominion of investors trading only in nine-figure increments (yes, we're talking millions).

Would it surprise you to learn that, according to the Bank for International Settlements, investors trade some $4 trillion worth of foreign currencies every single day? But no physical exchange of currencies ever takes place. A stack of euros is not swapped for a stack of yen. No currency can be traded alone. It takes two to tango: a seller from one country and a buyer from another.

But remember, we said there's no physical exchange, either. The transactions take place over the counter. Dealers and traders exchange currencies with each other, either over the phone or using electronic-trading platforms where bid offers are posted and trades made.

How Currency Trading Works

When buying and selling money, the transaction is as simple as purchasing one currency and paying for it with another — or selling a currency and receiving payment for it in another country's currency. Let's say you are a currency trader. You think that the U.S. dollar is going to get stronger (the technical term is to "appreciate"). You then must decide what other country's currency the dollar will appreciate against, because no currency can increase in relation to itself. It's always relative to another.

If you are a currency trader and you think the American economy is pulling ahead of the Eurozone's, what should be your call? Easy: Buy dollars and pay for them with euros. (If you prefer, you can think of it like selling euros).

How do you make profit? When the dollar appreciates, simply buy back the euros you sold and pay for them with the dollars you bought. You'll end up purchasing more euros with your dollars because the dollar is worth more. Your profit is the additional euros you buy.

Is your head spinning yet? To those experienced at foreign currency trading, it's no more complicated than buying and selling shares of stock, but it can be confusing for newcomers. For example, the U.S. dollar may have become stronger than the euro, but that doesn't mean the dollar has become stronger than the British pound. The dynamic between the pound and the U.S. dollar may be entirely different.

Next time you are in a Walmart or Target store, just check out where things are made. The first thing you will notice is how few items are made in the U.S. Next you will notice how many things are made in China. Years ago, it was Japan, Taiwan or Mexico. All of that has to do with the value of currency. It is naïve to think these movements cannot affect our personal wealth. We operate in a global economy. It's all interconnected — the strength of the dollar, overseas manufacturing, the shrinking U.S. industrial base, the national debt. You may not be able to change any of it, but seeing the global picture should point you toward a more conservative investing pattern as you approach retirement.

Political Risk

Those who think politics can't affect their wealth are naïve. Politicians make decisions every day that affect your personal wealth in some form or other. When the stock market crashed in 2008, the finger-pointing began almost immediately. Most blamed the Federal Reserve. The Fed is responsible for regulating the lending institutions who issued the bad loans that were at the heart of the mess. One can certainly make an argument that the national economy would never have experienced the woes it did had the Fed had a tighter rein on lending,

Talk about irony: The FCIC (Financial Crisis Inquiry Commission) was created by the U.S. government to investigate the cause of the 2008 stock market crash, and the commission pointed the finger of blame squarely back at the U.S. government. The FCIC made its findings known in January 2011, describing a house of cards. The housing bubble was brought on by easy money (low interest rates) and "scant regulations." To whom do the regulators report? Congress! Obviously the lawmakers on Capitol Hill (and the law enforcers under their supervision) were either asleep at the wheel or looking the other way when banks began their ill-advised lending practices.

What is plain in hindsight is how trillions of dollars in shaky mortgage contracts became a virus that spread through the national economy like a cancer. The bad loans came first. Then securities that were collateralized by those bad loans. These mortgage-backed securities were then marketed and purchased by investors around the world. The membrane containing the pressure of an over-inflated housing market finally couldn't take it any longer in 2007. The chickens circling the hen house started coming home to roost. The collapse of small banks had a ripple effect right up the line until finally the entire house of cards imploded, costing the American economy as much as $30 trillion by some estimates.

When the FCIC filed its report, the commission said the government "lacked the political will" to hold lending institutions accountable for their errant judgment and misdeeds. Why would that be the case? Could it be because of lobbying? According to the Center for Responsive Politics, a nonpartisan, nonprofit research group based in Washington, DC, the financial, insurance and real estate sector is the largest source of campaign contributions of all the lobbying groups. It spent $468.8 million on lobbying during the 2008 crash.

The entire 629-page report can be found online at by typing "FCIC financial crisis report" into just about any search engine. It is written in very plain language and clearly lays the blame for the crisis at the feet of the politicians and those who report to them.

That's just one example of how political risk can affect your wealth, and we haven't even mentioned the 800-pound gorilla in the room — taxes — or his 500-pound brother — monetary policy. Politicians control tariffs, wage levels, labor laws, environmental regulations and even the definition of "money." Make no mistake about it: What Congress decides to do, or not to do, today will affect your investments and your pocketbook tomorrow.

Business Risk

When it comes to navigating the minefield, business risk is one of the more obvious, but nonetheless dangerous, hazards. If you own investments that are linked to business (and which ones aren't, really) then risk is an inherent part of their makeup. There is the possibility that a company will have lower-than-anticipated profits, or that it will experience a loss rather than a profit. Business risk is influenced by numerous factors, including sales volume, per-unit price, input costs, competition, overall economic climate and government regulations.

In today's business world, companies hire professional analysts to calculate business risk. These people are paid high salaries to make recommendations to boards of directors regarding all of these potential land mines. Some companies use complex software with sophisticated mathematical capabilities to guide them through the choppy waters of business risk, and they still get it fatally wrong sometimes.

40

Most business startups, big or small, fail within five years of inception. Near where I live in the Toledo area, I drive by a location that has been home to at least four restaurants in as many years. Is there something about the location? While there appears to be no rhyme or reason for some business failures, others are doomed by any number of causal factors:

Technology: Polaroid is a good example of a huge company that was put out of business by a change in technology. It was so good at one time that the name was the product. No one said, "Hey, take an instantly developed photograph!" They said, "Take a Polaroid!" It's sort of like what Kleenex is to tissues and Band-Aid is to small bandages. But when you and I started taking digital pictures, the Polaroid executives refused to see the writing on the wall. The company, which went bankrupt in 2005, will forever exemplify not changing with the times.

Greed: Enron, once valued at $90 billion, is now kaput and synonymous with unbridled greed. The energy sector giant wasn't happy being a leader in its own universe. Enron started to dabble in internet commerce and exotic investment areas such as, of all things, weather futures. At one time the seventh-largest company in America, Enron went bankrupt in 2001, taking with it not only thousands of jobs but also the life savings of many retirees who had based their retirement accounts on the company's future. You can't say Enron without the accompanying mental picture of executives shredding documents and illegal shell companies.

Competition: Sony's Betamax video taping system was the hottest thing on the market when it first appeared in the late 1970s. The idea of recording a TV show and watching it later was intriguing enough for consumers to fork out in excess of $1,000 (more than $7,000 in today's dollars) to buy the machine. However, it soon had competition from JVC, with its brand of video cassette recorder, dubbed the VHS (Video Home System). The Sony product was technically superior when it came to clarity and quality, but JVC won the format war because it taped for up to six hours versus one hour for Betamax. If you wanted to tape a movie, you would run out of tape. The video rental business put the final nail in the Betamax coffin when it opted for the JVC format (most movies were at least an hour and a half long).

Poor Marketing: I could list thousands of business failures in this category, but one in particular that comes to mind is Flooz.com. Never heard of them? No wonder. It was an idea that just didn't have a chance —you could purchase so many credits of "internet currency" and redeem them in merchandise from online vendors. The only reason it got as far as it did was because of the dot-com frenzy of 2000 and 2001. Even though the startup had $50 million in marketing money to play with, owners of the company couldn't convince people that they needed another type of currency solely for the internet. Flooz.com hired Whoopi Goldberg to sell the idea via an ad campaign that was a notorious flop. All the advertising in the world couldn't overcome the basic question in consumers' minds, "Why not just use my credit card?" Then there was the name, which was a big turnoff. Flooz.com officially flopped in August 2001.

The list of failures goes on and on, but what you need to take away from this is that business risk is responsible for billions of dollars lost each year by entrepreneurs and the investors who back them. I am the last one to rain on anyone's parade if they want to take a risk in business. It's what America is all about. But since most end up in failure, it is a venue best suited for those who can afford to lose money. Investing in long shots is not the way to a happy, worry-free retirement.

Liquidity Risk

A liquidity risk is when you have a security or asset that cannot be traded quickly enough to avoid or minimize a loss. Some stock market trades are characterized by an unusually wide bid-ask spread. If that spread is small, the stock is very liquid. Traders can buy and sell it comfortably. If the spread is large, the stock is probably illiquid, meaning that buying and selling shares would be quite difficult since the amount buyers are looking to buy is a long ways away from what sellers are looking to sell.

Some view their assets in a brokerage account as liquid — almost as liquid as a bank account. Need your cash? Just sell off some of your holdings. But what happens if you are stuck with thousands of shares of a stock and there are no buyers — or no buyers willing to pay what you are asking? Depending on how deep your position is, a large price movement downward can spell potential disaster.

The rule of thumb is that the smaller the size of the security or its issuer, the larger the liquidity risk. That is why liquidity risk is generally associated with micro-cap and small-cap stocks or securities. That is not *always* the case, however, as the last two major market tumbles taught us. Liquidity risk rose to an abnormally high level during the 2000 market crash and the global financial crisis of 2008. When panic sets in, liquidity risk becomes a self-fulfilling prophecy: frantic investors try to sell their holdings at any price, causing market hysteria, an ever-widening bid-ask spread and large price declines.

As you approach retirement, the volatility of the market can be a trap from which you may not be able to extricate yourself if the timing is wrong. Instead, consider limiting your exposure to such risk by exploring alternative investing strategies that will not place your retirement income sources in jeopardy.

Advisor Risk

We want to believe that the medical professionals we trust with our lives are sane and reasonable, and I'm sure that most of them are. I spent several years in the medical profession and I can tell you firsthand that I had no experiences that would cause me to think otherwise. Not only were those whom I worked with and around sane and reasonable; they were skilled, caring individuals who put their patients' needs ahead of their own, often working long hours to make sure patients received the best care they could give. I have absolute confidence in the doctors who have treated me and my family. But no profession is without its wackos and renegades, and from what I read and hear, there are not many in the medical field, but that number is still greater than zero.

Don't make me say his name, but there is one doctor who comes on TV and gives advice that sometimes makes headlines because it's, well, just "out there." For example, pills that have the same effect as a facelift and secret cellulite remedies are touted in all seriousness. And this guy is a real doctor — a surgeon, in fact — who traded in his scrubs for the klieg lights after getting national attention on a syndicated talk show. But dispensing advice to a mass audience on what to swallow or smear on their skin has come at a price that involves attorneys and courtrooms.

Just as zany medical advice can be harmful to your health, bad financial advice can be harmful to your wealth. For example, not all financial advisors are alike: There is a difference between stockbrokers and investment advisors. Not all financial advisors bear the same legal responsibility to act in your best interests. There are essentially two legal standards that apply to the delivery of financial advice:

Suitability.
Fiduciary.

As this is written, stockbrokers are held to the suitability standard; this means their recommendations must be suitable for you based on your age, risk tolerance and financial situation. If they have their choice of several products, all suitable for your situation, they may recommend the one that pays them the most in fees and commissions. Keep in mind, this may not be the product that is best for your situation, but as long as it is suitable, that's OK. Stockbrokers do not have an obligation to educate you about other choices you may have.

A Registered Investment Advisor, on the other hand, is required by law to meet a more stringent *fiduciary* standard. The word comes from a Latin word meaning true, worthy of trust. A fiduciary has a legal responsibility to put your best interests ahead of all others in all aspects of the financial relationship.

Dana Anspach, in a Money Over 55 article entitled "The Cost of Bad Financial Advice," tells the horror story of a couple who didn't understand the difference in these two standards and picked the wrong advisor — a mistake that, according to Anspach, cost them more than $150,000 over seven years in fees and missed investment returns.

"The advisor they picked worked for a large national brokerage firm," wrote Anspach. "He did not take the time to educate the client about risk and return and the benefits of a diversified portfolio. Instead, he put them into a product that met their expressed need. A few years later when they were not happy, he put them in to a different product. A few years later, once again, a new product. All of these products met the suitability standard. The client had invested $500,000. The result of all those transactions: over $75,000 of commissions to the advisor. The result to the client: they did not lose money, but they did not make much either. Their account grew at about a 2 percent rate of return to a total of $575,000 after seven years."

How would an advisor with fiduciary responsibility have differed? Typically, a fiduciary will take the time to educate clients and determine what investment strategy is best for them — usually a diversified approach tailored to the client's age and proximity to retirement irrespective of any remuneration the advisor may receive.

I recommend that when you are searching for financial advice, you ask how the advisor gets paid. That will tell you a great deal about where an advisor's loyalty lies.

Owning Your Financial Future

One couple who came to my office shortly after the 2008 stock market meltdown owned a small business that was doing very well. They were so involved in the operation of their enterprise that they had no time to pay attention to the wealth they were accumulating. They had an investment account. That's all they knew, or wanted to know. They were "leaving it to the professionals," they said. When the market crash occurred, they lost more than a third of their fortune because all of their money was at inordinate risk.

The lesson they learned was painful but useful. The best steward of your financial affairs will always be you. That doesn't mean that you won't benefit by seeking professional help. You will. But know where your money is and why it is there. Make sure the financial professional advising you tells you where your money is, why it is there and what it is doing.

In the 21st century, we all must face the reality that things are not as they have always been. If you are reading this book, you are to be commended. Education is the first step in owning your financial future and dealing with modern risks that accompany investing. Knowing risks are there is half the solution. Knowing what to do about them is the other half.

CHAPTER FOUR

The Great Balancing Act

"Fear isn't an excuse to come to a standstill.
It's the impetus to step up and strike."
– Arthur Ashe

As was his custom, amateur astronomer Richard Carrington on the morning of Sept. 1, 1859, climbed the stairs leading to his private observatory, which was attached to his country estate outside of London. He opened the dome's shutter and was greeted by a clear blue sky. As was also his custom, he first pointed his huge brass telescope toward the sun to observe any changes. The first thing Carrington noticed was an unusually large cluster of dark spots on the surface of the sun. Then he saw what he later described as "two patches of intensely bright and white light" erupting from the sunspots. The phenomenon lasted for five minutes and then the eruptions suddenly vanished.

A few hours later, however, sparks began showering from telegraph machines. Suddenly, communications around the world began to fail. There were reports of colorful auras illuminating the night skies. Observers said the mysterious lights glowed so brightly that birds began to chirp, imagining that dawn had come early. Even farm workers rose early to start their daily chores, believing the sun had risen. Some familiar with the end-times prophecies of the Bible thought the end of the world was at hand.

What Carrington's telescope had spotted, however, was the real cause for the disturbances on earth: a massive solar flare with 10 billion times the energy released when the first atom bomb dropped on Hiroshima, Japan, in 1945. The solar flare belched electrified gas and subatomic particles toward the Earth, resulting in a geomagnetic storm that was named the "Carrington Event" after the man who observed it through his telescope. It was the largest geomagnetic solar storm science has recorded so far in the history of planet earth.

Scientists say we are overdue for another massive solar storm like the Carrington Event. Can you imagine what would happen if such a thing happened today? According to a 2008 report from the National Academy of Sciences, it could cause "extensive social and economic disruptions" due to its effect on power grids, satellite communications and GPS systems — and it would cost between $1 trillion and $2 trillion. Communications satellites would be knocked offline. Every time you buy gasoline and insert your credit card into the machine, a satellite handles the transaction. Can you imagine the chaos that would ensue if major financial transactions could not be transmitted?

We have come to rely on GPS systems for everything from air traffic control to space travel. That would all go haywire. Flights between North America and Asia, over the North Pole, would have to be rerouted. The biggest impact would be on that modern marvel we have come to know as the power grid, and experts warn that the grid is not ready. In 2008, the National Academy of Sciences stated that an 1859-level storm could knock out power in parts of the northeastern and northwestern United States for months, even years, forcing millions of Americans to revert to a pre-electric lifestyle or relocate. Water systems would fail and food would spoil. Thousands could die as a result of another solar storm like the one Carrington saw in 1859.

Feeling the Fear and Going Ahead

I don't know if reading about the Carrington Event gave you the shivers, but researching it and writing about it kind of made the hairs on my arm stand on end. But I concluded that, like so many things, there is not one thing I can do about it. If it happens, it happens. Could another massive solar geomagnetic storm knock out the power grid and kick us back into the Stone Age for a year or two? Maybe. But it falls into the "accept the things I cannot change" category.

The market crash of 2008 and similar economic events are a different matter. No, there is nothing I can personally do to prevent such a thing from recurring, but just as the sun's activity is cyclical, so is the stock market's behavior. We have had crashes before and we will have them again. If someone is ignorant to that, then the 2008 meltdown should have been a shot across the bows.

While there is nothing any of us can personally do to prevent such an event from recurring, we can analyze our portfolio and the universe of our personal financial assets and take steps to protect ourselves from another such economic disaster. Just as balance is the key to one walking a literal tightrope, balance is the key to our surviving financially in an unstable and shaky economic world.

One point I like to make when I conduct the pro bono educational seminars on investing and preparing for retirement is this: "It's not what happens in life; it's how we respond to what happens in life." That is true physically, emotionally, mentally, spiritually and in particular financially. For example, how do we keep our balance financially with elements of the economy that are, at the time of this writing, poised to upset our equilibrium?

Does it matter that:

- The U.S. has a half-trillion dollar trade deficit?

- The federal deficit is $17 trillion and counting?

- Consumer debt-to-income levels are the highest in history?

- Jobs are being outsourced to India, China, Mexico and other countries?

- We relatively recently experienced one of worst banking crises history and may be facing another?

- Manufacturing plants have moved and are moving to China and other developing nations?

- The U.S. dollar has lost 40 percent of its value in the last three decades?

- Raw product prices are generally increasing, indicating that inflation is returning?

- The nation's infrastructure in many areas of the country is in dire need of repair?

- At some point it is likely that the U.S. will experience another significant terrorist attack?

Yes, of course it matters. All these things matter. Feel the fear, but, since you can't change it, why not go forward, doing something positive to improve (financially or otherwise) your little corner of the world? Take steps to insulate and protect your retirement nest egg. Do everything for a reason when it comes to your investments. Know the why and the how long of your investments. When you face decisions regarding your personal finances, keep your balance and use your assets wisely.

The Rule of 100

Investors need to ask themselves how much risk they can take. The place to start is to start is with your age. One rule of thumb is the "rule of 100." It's not so much a *rule* as it is a *guideline.* The way it works is, take your age and put a percent sign after it. That's the portion of your money you should have in safe investments where your principal is protected from loss. After you have established an emergency fund to cover your expenses for eight months to a year, the rest can be placed in investments that contain risk. The emergency fund, by the way, is there for... well... emergencies. Your roof could need replacing. You may have a loved one who needs bailing out. You could lose your job or become ill or have an accident. The emergency fund needs to be liquid so you can access it with a check or at an ATM.

What do "low risk," "medium risk" or "high risk" investments really mean? The question you need to answer is, "Can I lose my money?" Then classify investment risk on a scale of one to five, with one being lowest possibility of loss and five representing highest possibility of loss (you could lose all of your money). Why would anyone risk loss? To have the opportunity to earn a higher rate of return. Risk does not *equal* return, but it does equal the *possibility* of return.

What I have observed over the years is that, with most people, it is human nature to be inherently over-optimistic. We will take to the highway in inclement weather confident that we will return home safely. Soldiers go to war, placing themselves in grave danger (is there any other kind?) but don't expect to be a casualty. When humans invest in the stock market, they fully expect their investment to pay off, not lose. When the market of 2008 occurred, many were downright shocked when they lost such a significant portion of their portfolios so quickly.

You take on higher levels of investment risk for the opportunity to earn a higher rate of return than what you can receive using only low-risk investments. This makes sense. Yet, if you don't understand the risks your money is exposed to, it can catch you off guard and instead of making more, you'll end up losing. Understanding the following categories, and the investment returns you might expect from each, will help you avoid unnecessary investment risk.

ARE YOU
OFF BALANCED?

There are only so many places you can put your money. The above illustration highlights some of the most common options and divides them into two categories — possible loss and no loss. As you can see, the investments on the right are with banks and insurance companies and the investments on the left are stock market-type investments. As the fulcrum in the middle suggests, the key to maintaining a healthy portfolio is to remain balanced. A theme you will hear repeated often in this book is that the older you get and the closer you are to retirement, the more conservative you need to be in your investment choices.

Using Money Correctly

There are two issues to be considered with our use of money: tax and risk. Notice that the arrows in the adjoining illustration go from left to right. The point is that we should always use taxable money first — money that creates interest and dividends and is already exposed. Then use tax-deferred money — money that is partially exposed. You should use pre-tax (qualified) money last — IRAs, 401(k)s, 403(b)s, TSAs, money purchase plans, profit sharing plans or simplified employee pension plans.

When people visit the offices of Generations Financial Group, we do a complimentary review of their overall financial health (I call it a financial check-up). I quite often see that they are using their qualified money when they have taxable money available for use. When I ask them why they are doing that, I usually get an answer similar to this one:

"Well Sam, I rolled over my IRA and that is where most of my money is, so I thought I should just start using it."

To put it mildly, that is an imprudent use of money. How would you answer this question: Of all the money you have, how much of it do you want to expose to the federal and the state government? I'm sure you got the right answer — as little as possible! So why expose money until you are ready to use it? John D. Rockefeller had it right. His rule was, "Don't pay taxes on money you are not using."

What about the other issue, risk? As we have said before, the older you get, the less risky you should be with your money. Which money should you use first in retirement? The riskier money — the money in the market. Then use money carefully selected from non-market investments. Lastly, use your guaranteed money. You know that money will be there when you get to it. You may not be able to say the same about your other holdings.

WHICH MONEY DO YOU USE? THE GROUND RULES:

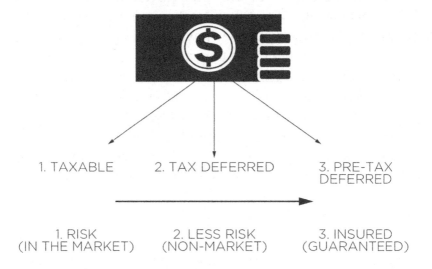

1. TAXABLE	2. TAX DEFERRED	3. PRE-TAX DEFERRED

1. RISK (IN THE MARKET)	2. LESS RISK (NON-MARKET)	3. INSURED (GUARANTEED)

By the way, regarding your 401(k): If you are 59 ½ or older, you may want to think about rolling it over as soon as possible. Many in our profession believe pensions and 401(k)s may be a target of the federal government to help fund its excessive spending. Regarding pensions, more and more companies (Ford and GM, for example) are offering a lump sum pension payout option to their retirees who are already receiving a monthly payout. If you are extended such an offer, consider taking it. That way *you* are able to control the *use* of that money. With a pension, you receive it as regular income and it is taxed as ordinary income, which means that it counts toward the formula used to determine whether you will pay taxes on your Social Security. A pension is not usually eligible for an IRA rollover unless they offer an option for a lump sum. Once the election is made it is usually irrevocable. You also need to know that (1) when electing a lump sum payout, you must be concerned about withholding. To avoid that 20 percent snatch, you must be prepared to roll over the lump sum directly into a qualified plan. (2) You must also ensure the continued tax-deferred growth of the unused portion. Remember: Don't pay tax on money you are not using. (3) You want to make sure you maintain investment control, positioning your money for a *reason,* knowing the *what, why* and *how long*.

Special Tax Options

The advantages to the lump-sum option should be pretty obvious. By exercising that option, you have the ability to build an inflation hedge with the money you now control. You also would have an emergency cash reserve; you could take whatever money you need to cover life's little (or big) surprises. Can you imagine staying in a pension and having an emergency situation where cash is required? You call your pension administrator and say, "Please advance me six months of my pension; I have an emergency." Not a chance.

Remember, once you decide, you can't undecide. But staying with the pension option means giving up a legacy for your family. A premature death means a loss of funds no matter how much it would have represented if it were a lump sum.

LUMP SUM
VS.
PENSION

INFLATION HEDGE	YES	NO
EMERGENCY CASH RESERVES	YES	NO
FLEXIBLE INCOME PAYMENTS	YES	NO
INVESTMENT CONTROL	YES	NO
MONEY FOR SURVIVORS (LEGACY)	YES	NO

CHAPTER FIVE

Increased Income from Reduced Taxes

"Fear can keep us up all night long,
but faith makes one fine pillow."
– Philip Gulley

One of the best investments you can make is tax savings. Every dollar you save in tax is better than a 100 percent return. If you don't save every dollar you are entitled to, that money is gone forever and all the earning power goes right with it for the rest of your life. But if you save it, it keeps growing for you. There are so many ways to save on your taxes, especially for those on Social Security.

Many on Social Security just accept their tax bill as inevitable. Wasn't it Benjamin Franklin who quipped, "The only two things that are certain in life are death and taxes"? Many people suppose that if one of those two inevitable twins has to pay a visit, they would rather have taxes knock on their door. But there are ways to legally and ethically avoid overpayment of taxes if you are acquainted with the strategies that are provided by the IRS itself in its very own code book. But you have to know where to look — that's the key.

Tax-Saving Strategies

In 1986, as part of tax reconciliation legislation, Congress created Section 42 of the IRS code, also known as "affordable housing" legislation. This new law allowed for significant dollar-for-dollar tax credits for investing in certain low-income housing buildings. I was able to help my clients save thousands of dollars by simply taking advantage of the provisions of that new law. Unfortunately, that ship has sailed and those provisions are no longer available. But if they ever come back around, we will be ready. The point is, this was a good, albeit short-lived tax provision made available by Congress but not widely advertised. You have to know where to look and stay plugged in to catch these opportunities to save on taxes. Several years ago, an 82-year-old man who was a regular listener to my radio show came to me for a personal review. The first place I usually start is with the latest tax return. When I looked at his total calculated tax, it was $4,800, but his total tax liability was only $200. He was taking advantage of the IRS code, section 42 and had $4,600 in tax credits. I commended him.

"I hate paying taxes," he explained, adding that since he retired he had made a hobby out of reading everything he could get his hands on pertaining to tax credits. He is one of the exceptions. Most people remain oblivious of the many tax strategies that are hiding in plain sight in the IRS code.

Some have reduced their tax liability significantly by changing their dividend investments. Take, for example, someone on Social Security who has significant investments in taxable sources and mutual funds. With mutual funds and bond funds, any interest, dividends and capital gain distributions are usually reinvested. In other words, the IRS considers these distributions and dividends reportable personal income, even though you did not see the money and did not spend the money.

This type of income is considered "phantom income" for that reason. You still receive a 1099 and you are taxed as if it were a paycheck you received in the mail. Ironically, in 2008, after years of paying taxes on this phantom income, some experienced a dramatic decline in the value of their asset. In other words, they paid lots of taxes on money they never had the pleasure of spending. Adding insult to injury, those dividends and

58

Sam Foreman

distributions may have been just enough to push them into the taxable zone on their Social Security.

Some think that by moving their funds to tax-free bonds and tax-free mutual bond funds, they solve a tax problem. Often the reality is that the interest they receive, although tax free, still counts against them in the calculation used to determine tax on Social Security income.

As a side note, one person told me how great his advisor was because he moved all of his IRA to tax-free municipal bonds so he could get tax-free IRA money. I had to break the news to him that anything you put into a traditional IRA will be taxed when it comes out!

Tax on Social Security

Some who are new to Social Security are surprised to learn that if they earn over a certain amount they must pay income tax on a portion of their Social Security. It wasn't always that way. In 1935, when President Franklin D. Roosevelt first signed the Social Security Act into law, it was not considered taxable income. It was during the presidency of Ronald Reagan that the Social Security Amendments of 1983 were passed, enacting the following changes:

- A single taxpayer whose income from all sources plus one half of his or her Social Security exceeds $25,000 will start paying tax on up to 50 percent of his or her Social Security benefits, or...

- A married couple whose income from all sources plus one half of their Social Security exceeds $32,000 will start paying tax on up to 50 percent of their Social Security benefits.

The next tax increase would come with the 1993 budget deal under President Bill Clinton, which raised taxation to up to 85 percent of benefits for single filers with the same calculated values incomes of more than $34,000, and for couples with annual incomes of $44,000 or more. As this is written, the law still reads that way.

There are strategies that can be used to in some cases limit, or even eliminate, Social Security taxes. It depends on how much income you earn in addition to your Social Security benefits and whether that income is considered reportable by the IRS. One possible solution is to move assets from the reportable category to the nonreportable category by replacing phantom income with carefully selected liquid master limited partnership (MLP) stocks where the dividends are mostly tax deferred, and therefore not considered by the IRS as reportable income. This strategy has the potential of double and triple tax savings.

Another strategy is to replace accounts that generate traditional interest and dividends (reportable income) with tax-deferred annuities (nonreportable income). The value of using a strategy such as this becomes obvious when you consider that every dollar you save in taxes is better than a 100 percent return. It is helpful to see a before-and-after comparison using a "what-if" test in a tax-reduction analysis report.

Energy Offset Conversions

Another example of a tax-reduction strategy is energy-offset conversion. When I examine tax returns as part of an overall financial evaluation, I quite often see a large increase in tax for a particular year because the client sold real estate or a business, or had a large capital gain because they sold a large amount of stock. We can't rewind the clock in those cases, where no offset strategy was in place in the year of those income-generating transactions, but with a little advance planning, much of this tax can be eliminated.

One recent case had to do with a man who had just sold off his positions in storage units. He received $400,000 and a reportable gain of $200,000. Understandably, he was concerned about what that was going to do to his tax liability. Fortunately for him, we had time before the end of the year to employ an offset strategy. My first question to him was how much of the $200,000 he needed. His response was that he did not need any of the money. He had more than enough to meet his needs. Good answer! We were able to find a fully first-year deductible energy program. (Note: Not all energy programs are 100 percent deductible.)

He was able to take an equal amount of his reportable gain, $200,000, and put it into the program. On his tax return, he would have to report the $200,000 as a gain, but on line 17 of that same return, he would able to subtract $200,000, thus successfully offsetting the tax liability. He still had his other $200,000 to do with as he wished; however, his new deductible investment would not likely produce income for six to nine months, which was not an issue for him. This strategy involves registered securities and a knowledgeable, licensed securities representative, along with a tax service familiar with this strategy.

Using a 1031 Exchange

Another tax-reduction case involved an elderly couple who owned a sizeable amount of real estate, which they had been using as rental property. The property was valued at over $500,000. Their rental returns were averaging 3 percent, or $15,000 per year, most of which was taxable. Now they wanted to sell the property. They had received an acceptable offer, but if they sold the property, they would be hit with an enormous capital gains tax. They knew their son would eventually inherit the real estate and would enjoy a step-up in basis and pay no capital gains tax. The solution to the couple's dilemma in this case was to arrange a starker 1031 exchange (Internal Revenue Code Section 1031) for them. We were able to facilitate an exchange, placing the proceeds of the sale with a large real estate company specializing in 1031s. As a result, they were able to sell their real estate, pay no tax by deferring the tax indefinitely, more than double their returns with tax-favored treatment — and still not lose the advantage of a step-up in value for their son.

Tax-Deferred Annuities

A conservative approach that is very popular with those approaching retirement or in retirement these days is tax-deferred annuities. One reason for heightened interest in this strategy is because of the safety of these instruments. One couple who had most of their money in tax-free municipal bonds found that they were able to eliminate the tax on their Social Security income altogether by switching to simple tax-deferred annuities. Unlike tax-free income, which can actually cause taxes on Social Security income, annuities have no effect. By making the switch, they also eliminated the interest rate risk associated with municipal bonds. In short, annuities are a simple way to reduce taxes by offering tax-deferred growth. Their benefits include:

- No 1099 at end of year.

- Not reporting income.

- Saving on taxes.*

- No effect on Social Security income.

*With tax-deferred annuities, taxes will be due at the time of distribution. If distributions are taken prior to age 59 ½, an additional 10 percent federal tax penalty will apply.

CHAPTER SIX

Not All Annuities Are Created Equal

"There is nothing brilliant or outstanding in my record, except perhaps this one thing: I do the things that I believe ought to be done, and when I make up my mind to do a thing, I act." –
Theodore Roosevelt

Perhaps no word in the glossary of financial terms has more misinformation swirling around than does the simple word "annuity." Some financial advisors swear by them, and some swear at them. What is it about this little word that generates so much controversy in financial advisory circles?

From time to time, when I am called upon to speak to a group on the subject, I like to try an experiment. Standing before the whiteboard, marker in hand, I ask the group to list off the attributes of the perfect investment. When we boil it down it usually looks something like this:

High rate of return with complete safety: Double digits preferred but at least a better-than-average return that follows the stock market when it goes up but not when it goes down. Principal guaranteed.

Full liquidity: Get your money out of the investment at any time without paying a penalty for early withdrawal.

Tax free: Pay no taxes at all on either the gains while they are accruing or the money you withdraw from the investment.

Of course, such an investment does not exist. In the investing world, there are tradeoffs. It reminds me of a sign I saw in a small grocery store in rural Ohio one time: *"**Good Service, High Quality, Low Prices** — **Pick any Two.**"*

With investments, higher interest rates are usually accompanied by a longer term of investment, which is why a five-year CD yields more than a one-year CD. Shorter-term investments with great liquidity are usually accompanied by lower rates of return. Higher returns come with higher risk.

There is no "free lunch" and there is no "perfect investment." Once the group agrees on that idea, I like to describe an investment on the board without giving it a name. I call it *"Investment Alpha."*

"Investment Alpha" will provide substantial returns with little or no downside risk. Your returns will be linked to the performance of an index, such as the S&P 500, the Dow Jones Industrial Average, or the NASDAQ, or maybe even a combination of indices. Your account will rise in value when as those indices rise, up to a cap of, say 6 to 10 percent. When the market falls, your gains are locked in and you can never go backwards.

"Investment Alpha" is also tax deferred — that is, you owe no taxes on your gains as long as you keep the investment contract and do not withdraw money from it. This allows the money you would have paid in taxes to continue to grow at compounded interest. You will pay taxes on the money you withdraw from the contract, and it will be taxed as ordinary income.

"Investment Alpha" is guaranteed so that you never lose your principal due to market volatility. If the market crashes, the worst your account can do is zero. You don't have to worry about losing your nest egg during a market crisis such as the one we had in 2008.

"Investment Alpha" has no fees. No fees on the front door and no fees on the back door. No maintenance fee, no investment fees, no hidden fees and no trading commissions. The only fee you would pay is a nominal fee, perhaps a few basis points (less than a percent), if you elected to have an optional rider to guarantee you a lifetime income that you couldn't outlive.

"Investment Alpha" is transferrable to your named beneficiaries upon your death. Any unused portion of the investment is left to heirs *probate free*. It would not be tax-free, like a life insurance death benefit, but it would be taxed as ordinary income upon withdrawal.

By the time we have described in detail how "Investment Alpha" works, nearly everyone wants to know where to sign up for one.

"By a show of hands, how many would favor an investment like this?" I ask.

Nearly every hand goes up.

"Now, by a show of hands, how many here like annuities?"

Only a few hands go up, and, as it turns out, those are people who have annuities and are pleased with their performance.

When I tell the group that the real name of "Investment Alpha" is a fixed index annuity there is obvious surprise and a few astonished looks.

It does go to show how preconceived notions can influence our investing decisions. Brokers, Wall Street mavens and the media moguls they support tend to typecast annuities, giving them a bad name, not because these products aren't worthwhile or effective, but because they (the Wall-Street crowd) don't market them. It's like asking a Ford dealer to rate Chevys.

This is not surprising. A 2010 study conducted by Allianz Life Insurance Company of North America found in a survey of people between the ages of 44 and 70, 54 percent of those polled expressed a dislike for annuities. But the same survey also found that only 7 percent said they have kept up with new annuity products now offered. What does that tell you? They don't know what they don't know.

It reminds me of a commercial that aired sometime back that was famous for its catchphrase, "This isn't your father's Oldsmobile." In the 1970s, the Oldsmobile was a known as a big sedan, a gas-guzzler family car. The Buick had its signature three or four holes on the front fenders. With the Oldsmobile, it was rockets: rockets on the hood, rockets on the fenders, rockets on the steering wheel and rockets on the gaudy chrome trim. By the late 1980s, people had changed their buying habits and the Oldsmobile was losing market share.

General Motors retooled and came out with the Cutlass Supreme a sassy, smaller car that was sure to bring the buyers back into the showroom. But it wasn't happening. The advertising people had to come up with something that in 15-seconds would open the public's eyes. They heard the word "Oldsmobile" and it was game over. Their mental picture was that of a stodgy old sedan with gaudy chrome rockets. To re-establish the brand for the younger audience, the ad people came up with a short film of the perky Cutlass zipping along with fun-loving young people all around. At the end of each spot, the voice-over say, "This is *NOT* your father's Oldsmobile."

Like General Motors, insurance companies completely retooled annuities in the early 2000s. But the old impressions still linger, as the Allianz survey revealed. Interestingly, when the poll-takers asked the question similar to mine — that is, what they would like your perfect investment to look like — 69 percent preferred a product guaranteed not to lose value. When offered a choice between an investment with a 4 percent return and a guarantee not to lose value and an investment that returned 8 percent but was exposed to loss, 80 percent of those surveyed preferred the former.

When you Google the word "annuity," you come up with more misinformation than lies at a tall tales contest. To find out why, just follow the money trail. Most of the advertisements that pay for the articles are funded by brokerage houses. The "experts" know little about modern annuities and how they work because they don't market them. Naturally they would not extol the virtues of anything that was not part of their profit picture.

Annuities are like automobiles. There are many car manufacturers and many types within those makes of automobile. A big, four-door sedan is a car. A little two-seater sports car is a car. But they are not alike. Likewise, when you see the word, "annuity," ask what type of annuity you are talking about.

There are five basic types of annuities:

- Immediate.

- Fixed.

- Fixed index.

- Variable.

- Hybrid.

"Hybrid" annuities are added to that list because they combine some of the features of the other types of annuities listed.

Fixed and fixed index annuities may be a great foundational choice for retirement because of their attributes of safety, predictable performance and tax-favored status. Returns from annuities are tax-deferred: You don't pay taxes until you withdraw them.

Just as the term "automobile" describes sports cars as well sports utility vehicles, the word "annuity" is a broad umbrella term under which we can find a variety of financial instruments with different mechanics, features and benefits — yet they are all annuities. What all annuities have in common, however, are that they are issued by insurance companies that guarantee the principal, they typically allow you to defer taxes on gains until you make a withdrawal, and they are generally not subject to probate (state laws vary).

Annuities in History

The ancient Romans invented annuities. They called them "annua," which is Latin for "annual stipends." Soldiers would pool their money and if they were killed in battle the agreed-upon portion of the money pool would either be paid to the soldier's widow in a lump sum or given to her in annual payments, thus the term. The idea continued to exist in one form or another over the years, and came to America in 1759, when Presbyterian ministers were allowed to participate in an annuity to benefit their families.

The Pennsylvania Company for Insurance on Lives and Granting Annuities was the first to market the idea publicly in 1912. The old annuities had few moving parts and little financial horsepower, not like today's annuity contracts. They offered a guaranteed return of principal, a fixed rate of interest, a payout choice of (a) life or (b) a certain number of years. If you chose the set-year payout, you forfeited control of the account. In essence, you made a deal with the insurance company. If you died early, all the money went to the insurance company, not your heirs. If you chose a lifetime payout and proceeded to live a long time after taking that option, you certainly got the best of that deal.

By the dawn of the 21st century, when baby boomers began contemplating retirement, the insurance companies saw a need to take annuities back to the drawing board. The old-style annuities weren't that popular with boomers. They liked the idea of a guaranteed lifetime payout but didn't find the idea of forfeiting the balance of the account very attractive. Also, fixed interest rates were low in comparison to 1990s stock market returns.

Immediate Annuities

An immediate annuity is straightforward. You deposit a sum of money with an insurance company and immediately turn that deposit into an income stream. It could be for 10 years or it could be for as long as you live. The deposit spends no time in deferral gaining interest. The income you select stops when you die.

Variable Annuities

Variable annuities are stock market investments in an annuity wrapper. They were developed in 1952, primarily for the tax-deferred feature. The downside to variable annuities compared to their fixed annuity cousins is that variables can lose money. Another problem with variable annuities is their high fees and their use of mutual funds. They can be great in a booming stock market environment, but not so great when the market faces a downturn. They also come with high fees because mutual funds have both reportable inside fees and nonreportable trading fees. Variable annuities also have mortality/expense charges.

Fixed Annuities

A traditional fixed annuity has few bells and whistles. The interest rate is fixed, so you know what you will be earning, and there is a penalty for early withdrawal (before the surrender period expires). Fixed annuities resemble bank CDs in many ways, except for two major differences: Interest rates are typically double — if not triple — those of CDs and gains are tax deferred. Interest earned from a CD is taxable year by year. Surrender periods with traditional fixed annuities range between three and seven years.

We use the term "traditional" here because annuities have changed recently and the type of annuity we are describing here has been around for many years. These annuities ensure the safety of your principal, allow for tax deferment and can provide a guaranteed lifetime income. A few traditional fixed annuities come with income riders, but most require you to annuitize the contract to convert the balance into a lifetime income.

Index Annuities

Index annuities are sometimes called fixed index annuities (FIAs). Just like the traditional fixed annuity, they provide a minimum rate of interest (sometimes called a "floor"). The rate of return over that floor is based on a stock market index — such as the Dow or the S&P — thus the term "index" annuities. The insurance carrier sets a cap on this rate of return. You get a portion of the gains of the market, up to the cap, but you do not participate on the downturns. So if the index produces a 20 percent growth in a year, your gains will hit that cap and stop. On the other hand, if the index records a 20 percent loss, your gains are locked in yearly and your account balance remains the same. The caps are a tradeoff for having guarantee of principal.

Contracts vary from company to company, and these annuities can come with a bonus. Since insurance companies compete with brokerage houses, banks and other insurance companies for your money, bonuses help to attract customers. The insurance company adds an extra sum to the amount you deposit and this is included in your account balance. If the insurance company offers, say, a 7 percent bonus and you deposit $100,000, your account value is immediately $107,000.

Hybrid Annuities

Everyone knows what a hybrid car does — it combines electric power with gasoline power. Hybrid annuities are fixed index annuities with an optional income rider. The availability of an income rider changes the dynamics of the annuity so much that it is sometimes called an "income annuity."

Think of a motorcycle with a sidecar. If the motorcycle is the fixed index annuity, the sidecar is the guaranteed lifetime income rider. Like the motorcycle, the fixed index annuity can stand alone but the only way you can own an income rider is if it is attached to a standalone annuity.

These products have a few moving parts but the two main ones are:

Accumulation account
This is the actual account value of the annuity. Once the surrender period ends, this is the value you can walk away with (most surrender periods are 10 years but this varies from company to company).

Income account
This is a ledger account used to calculate the lifetime income provided by the income rider. It is not the actual value, or the walk-away value, of the contract.

These two accounts grow at different rates. The accumulation account may grow according to the performance of a stock market index such as the S&P 500. The income account grows at a rate fixed by the insurance carrier. The rate paid on the income base is called the "roll up" rate and is typically in the 7 to 8 percent range, but this also varies from carrier to carrier. Typically, the growth of the accumulation account is predicated on performance of an index while the growth of the income account is fixed.

Some insurance companies offer a bonus. Let's say the company offers an 8 percent bonus. That means if you deposit $100,000 into the annuity, you start off with $108,000. Your income account is credited with the bonus, too. The terms of these bonuses vary from carrier to carrier. Some are vested bonuses, and some are not.

The longer you let your income account grow, the higher your income and the older you are when you decide to start the income, the higher percentage of the income account you will receive. The formula is based on your attained age. A 75-year-old may receive a lifetime payout of 6.5 percent of the income account for the rest of his or her life. A 70-year-old may receive 6 percent of the income account value for life. Once income is triggered, the growth of the income account stops but the income continues for the rest of your life.

Before the advent of hybrid (income) annuities, the main sticking point for many baby boomers with fixed annuities was that you had to annuitize the contract to get a lifetime income payout. In those days, if you triggered your lifetime income and died soon thereafter, your heirs got nothing. The new hybrid annuities are much more appealing to 21st-century retirees. According to LIMRA, an insurance research organization, sales of fixed index annuities in 2013 were $39.3 billion, up 17 percent from the previous year, while sales of variable annuities fell by 1 percent.

Balance in All Things Financial

If there is one pure truth I have learned in all my years as both a medical and a financial professional, it is this: Beware of extremes, because the truth is usually in the middle. I have seen some clients come to me for help and every stitch of money is tied up in the market. They are nearing retirement and their portfolio is overweight with potentially crippling risk. Others are on the other end of the spectrum. They have squirreled their money away in CDs, every penny of it. Their money is on siesta! Then there are those who have put every bit of their retirement savings in annuities and often have no idea why. Perhaps they were "sold" the annuities by an insurance salesman out for a commission.

In all three cases, they need to balance out their portfolios strategically. There is a place for all three mediums of investment in a "smart" portfolio, but how much should go where depends on a number of factors. Proper balance is not achieved by impulsive or emotional decisions, but scientifically and mathematically.

CHAPTER SEVEN

The Need for a Solid Foundation

"Confront your fears, list them, get to know them, and only then
will you be able to put them aside and move ahead."
– Jerry Gille

On April 11, 1965 — Palm Sunday — an F4 tornado touched down a few miles from Toledo, Ohio. In a matter of minutes, the twister had taken the lives of 18 people and caused $25 million dollars in property damage.

Later, as news reports began to track the event, a total of 47 tornados had touched down across five states over an 11-hour period, creating one of the most violent tornado outbreaks ever recorded. Fierce winds had picked up cars and boats and thrown them into buildings like an angry 2-year-old throwing toys in a temper tantrum. Bricks, shingles and debris littered the ground. The wind had literally ripped houses apart; some had simply vanished with only their concrete foundations left behind to show where they once had stood.

Almost as soon as the storms had passed, families began milling around their devastated residences, poking through the debris and literally picking up the pieces of their lives. Only splinters remained of some houses, but their foundations were the bedrock from which they could begin anew. Today, you can drive down stretches of highway where the tornado hit and you would never know anything had happened, proving that as long as there is a good foundation, you can rebuild. Those virtually indestructible foundations serve as an apt metaphor for the base of a well-planned retirement portfolio. In planning for retirement, if we have our foundational investments locked in place with guarantees, then winds of stock market volatility can howl but they can't completely wipe us out. In building our financial house, we need a strong base that is impervious to erosion. Foundational investments securely support everything else we build upon them. In the PCP model, wealth management begins with a solid foundation.

Adjusting Our Expectations

Just as the materials to build a literal foundation are very different from the materials that we choose for our living space, so too, are the safe investments we choose for the base of our financial portfolio very different from the investments that we select for our growth and liquidity.

Think about it. If I were to ask you if you wanted to build your dream home out of 8-by-6-by-8 inch concrete blocks, you'd likely say no. That wouldn't make for an attractive home and it would be void of the flexibility, breathability and beauty that so many other building materials would supply.

That's how it is with our portfolio. I am not suggesting that we build a financial house out of foundational material. That would go against everything that I believe in: true diversity and noncorrelation. Let me explain.

When I am sitting at the conference table with a couple who has just retired, I usually see that most of their retirement money is invested in the stock market. When I ask them how much of their money at this point in their life they think should be insured, one of them will usually say, "all of it." That is a sensible reply, but the problem is they rarely have any of their money insured.

After some risk-tolerance tests, we try to make sure that a good percentage of their assets are placed in a hybrid annuity with a guaranteed income rider. This add-on provides a special income account with a guaranteed growth rate that accrues compound interest until they elect to begin receiving their income. Hybrid annuities with income riders have also been called "income" annuities because they are capable of providing an income that the annuitant cannot outlive with a legacy value for beneficiaries in the event of the annuitant's premature death.

The reason why annuity "anchors" make a good foundation for a well-constructed financial house is because, unlike banks, brokerage houses and mutual funds, insurance companies can pool risks. We can learn many lessons by examining history. In the Great Depression of the 1930s, people had difficulty getting money out of banks, brokerage houses and mutual funds. But if they were receiving monthly income from their insurance company, there was no interruption in the delivery of that check. Banks can leverage up to nine times the amount of your deposit and they can invest in almost anything. Insurance companies, however, are highly regulated and must keep a one-to-one ratio in reserves. In other words, they have to have an equal amount in reserve for every amount they have on deposit.

One of the most convincing arguments for using fixed index and hybrid annuities was the forth in the December 2010 study by the Wharton School of the University of Pennsylvania, one of the most respected business schools in the United States. They compared the performance of the S&P 500 index and fixed index annuities. In other words, the study looked at what would happen if you put all your money in the S&P 500 index, which is a market-based investment that can suffer losses, versus what would happen if you placed the same amount in a fixed index annuity, which is insured against the risk of loss.

ANNUALIZED FIVE-YEAR RETURNS

PERIOD	S&P RETURN	FIA AVG. RETURN	NUMBER OF FIA'S	RETURN RANGE
1997-2002	9.39%	9.19%	5	7.80 to 12.16%
1998-2003	-0.42%	5.46%	13	3.00 to 7.97%
1999-2004	-2.77%	4.69%	8	3.00 to 6.63%
2000-2005	-3.08%	4.33%	28	0.85 to 8.66%
2001-2006	5.11%	4.36%	13	1.91 to 6.55%
2002-2007	13.37%	6.12%	23	3.00 to 8.39%
2003-2008	3.18%	6.05%	19	3.00 to 7.80%
2004-2009	-1.05%	4.19%	27	2.25 to 6.83%

It comes down to *potential* versus *protection*. With the market, yes you have potential: the potential to lose a lot, (0 to -40 percent), and the potential to make a lot, (0 to +20 percent). But with the FIA (fixed index annuity), you have protection. You won't have the potential to make a lot, but you also won't lose anything. With your retirement money, which is more important? Remember, you can't write off losses in a retirement account; it must be safer.

POTENTIAL VS. PROTECTION

INDEXED ANNUITY

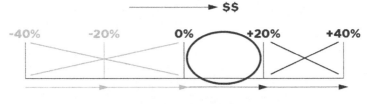

INVESTMENT

Below is the model that has protected many from the pitfalls of traditional pie chart-style of investing. We have already discussed the *foundation* of a portfolio. What about the rest?

TRUE DIVERSIFICATION NON-CORRELATED MODEL

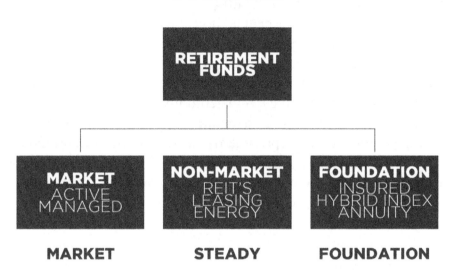

After laying a foundation with fixed index annuities, the next level in building this new non-correlated portfolio must be something that has a strong steady return, something that is tax favored for non-retirement funds, but something not affected by the market for both retirement and non-retirement funds. These are alternative registered investments such as non-traded real estate investment trusts (REITs), leasing programs, business development programs and energy programs, all of which require the assistance of a licensed securities representative to determine whether they are appropriate.

Several of the REITs on the market today started out as non-market and then went public or were bought out by a market REIT. My experience with these over the last 25 years has been that they include a holding period between 18 months and eight years (the longest one I held). This is one you don't want to do yourself. You will need an experienced securities representative to help you. The same would be true for non-market equipment leasing, business development programs, and energy programs, all of which are tax-favored investments with the aim of a **steady** return and without market volatility.

The last level of our financial house would logically be *market* investments. Speed is the main ingredient here. If you are near retirement or already retired, you need to be able to react immediately to changes in today's volatile market. The best way to approach this is to have a registered investment advisor representative with "skin in the game," so to speak. My market IRA is identical to my representative's IRA, along with hundreds of others. Whenever a change is made, we all change together in a fraction of a second and we all get the same price. We watch the account and make changes as they are needed.

Life Insurance

Truth is stranger than fiction. Who would guess that both concrete and life insurance were invented by the Romans around the 100 B.C.? In fact, the Pantheon and the Roman aqueducts are still standing to prove it. About the same time that these architectural feats were being created with the aid of a powdered limestone mixed with clay, sand and gravel, the idea of life insurance born. As was the case with annuities, the ancient Roman soldiers pooled their money in order to provide a proper burial for fallen comrades.

Insurance is another foundational material for our financial house. According to the 2013 Insurance Barometer Study by LIMRA, 70 percent of people 65 and older own life insurance. The same study found that "consumers without life insurance tend to be more concerned about everyday expenses than those with life insurance." Here are some functional reasons why we own life insurance:

Providing for our families: According to a 2013 Forbes article, "There's Only ONE Undisputable Reason to Buy Life Insurance," it all boils down to taking care of the people we love. The article stated: "There are people you love, your children, for example. You want to ensure they have a solid financial base (however you define it). The best answer is very often life insurance." The piece went on to explain that even if our life insurance is earmarked to pay estate taxes, pay funeral costs, or provide income for our loved ones, it all boils down to taking care of the people we love. It's a way to transfer a fine foundation to the next generation.

Funeral costs: Preplanned funerals prepaid with designated life insurance proceeds are becoming more and more popular. While the tendency might be to think that baby boomers want to control everything, including their burial, it's generally a matter of genuine concern that motivates the pre-payers. After all, anyone who has had to plan a funeral knows the angst of trying to please the deceased loved one. And loss of a family member evokes such strong emotions that it lends itself to emotional and excessive choices that might later be regretted. So pre-planning makes it easier on our heirs. They simply follow the game plan and enjoy the peace of mind that comes with knowing that everything was done to our liking. By the way, the average funeral costs about $6,000, with an additional $3,000 for the vault, liner and gravesite. Cremation? Around $3,700.

Planned giving: Policies are often purchased as our "going-away present" to our favorite university, church or other charity. We simply designate our charity as the named beneficiary and smile, knowing that we are taking care of the organizations that took care of us.

College funds: Grandparents today often play a significant role in the lives of their grandchildren, including securing college funds for their heirs. According to studies, the average cost of one year of college is about $3,000 for community college, $5,000 for a public university, and $22,000 for a private university. According to a 2014 Pew Research Center report, those with college degrees earn $17,500 more per year than those without one.

Taxes: Federal estate taxes and state inheritance taxes are often anticipated and cared for by life insurance proceeds. This prevents heirs from having to liquidate an investment at a less than optimal time to settle the estate.

Life Insurance in Retirement Planning

Investment-grade life insurance came along in the late 1970s. It's different from term insurance, which ends after a specific and predetermined length of time, such as 10, 15 or 20 years. And while investment-grade life is a type of permanent life insurance, it differs from the typical permanent policy.

The advantage of the traditional permanent policy is that your policy accumulates cash value while your face value (death benefit) and premium is locked in. Permanent insurance is always more expensive than an equivalent amount of term insurance purchased on the same day because you keep your permanent coverage as long as you pay your premiums, even if you later become uninsurable.

Investment-grade life insurance takes permanent insurance up a notch. Instead of a stingy 1 or 2 percent on cash values, carriers of investment-grade permanent insurance pay interest based on the U.S. Treasury bills or a stock market index, such as the S&P 500. The more popular form of the latter is indexed universal life insurance, or IUL. The hallmark characteristic of universal life is that the policy discloses all fees and charges, even mortality costs.

The Insurance Revolution

American consumers were beneficiaries of an insurance revolution of sorts that took place in the early 1980s. Those who can remember the crazy days of inflation in the late 1970s and early 1980s remember when interest rates soared to as much as 18 percent. Some boomers began asking questions about their permanent life policies. Cash values of these old-style policies were growing by 1 or 2 percent per year when banks were paying 15 percent on a CD!

Something just didn't seem right. Why were insurance companies benefiting from the high interest rates and yet were not sharing the profits with policyholders? The reason was that up until then, insurance companies were not required to disclose all the details of the policy. They held all the cards. But they were about to see an example of the free enterprise system at work. Disgruntled policyholders began cashing in their whole life policies, putting their money to work for double-digit interest. They bought cheap term life policies for the raw insurance feature they needed to protect their families.

Forced to compete, insurance companies fought back with investment-grade permanent policies: universal life (UL). Life insurance customers, many of them baby boomers approaching middle age, began coming back. They discerned that the rise in interest rates wouldn't last forever and that term policies, while temporarily cheaper, had expiration dates. They would have to undergo a new physical and pay much higher rates in 20 years if they wanted to keep the coverage. What if they became uninsurable then? Many of them didn't want to risk it.

The insurance companies had entered a new era of fairness and openness, some of it legislated, but most of it motivated by profit. These were good products. The more the consumer knew about them, the more attractive they would become, they figured. Before the index universal life policies came into being, returns on the cash value portions of these UL policies were based on the interest of U.S. Treasury bills. It was something that could be monitored, unlike the former arbitrary rates of traditional whole life policies. Premiums on UL policies were flexible, too. You could pay more into the policy when times were prosperous and pay less or even skip premiums when times were tough. You could also take withdrawals in the form of low-interest loans and death benefits remained tax free.

It didn't take long for boomers to realize the benefits of tax-deferred growth under the umbrella of these new investment-grade insurance policies. As investing mushroomed, the IRS passed new laws to prevent the tax benefits of investment-grade insurance from being abused. In 1982 the Tax, Equity, Fiscal, and Responsibility Act (TEFRA) was passed. Two years later, DEFRA, the Deficit Reduction Act, was passed. Then in 1988, TAMRA, Technical and Miscellaneous Revenue Act and the last of the regulatory triplets, was born.

When interest rates were high, people were dumping hundreds of thousands of dollars in premiums into these policies, letting them accrue tremendous amounts of cash value, borrowing against the policies and pocketing the money tax-free. TEFRA, DEFRA and TAMRA limited how much you could put into one of these new-fangled policies and still keep the tax-free status that the IRS afforded life insurance benefits.

When the stock market began to climb, the insurance companies preempted another boomer exodus and quickly created indexed universal life, or IUL. It was a big hit because it allowed boomers to benefit from bull (rising) markets while protecting them in bear (falling) markets. The novel idea of tying gains to a stock market index was met with acceptance as boomers voted with their checkbooks. Sales of this new type of policy, once people understood the value of it, soared.

IUL as a Foundation for Retirement

If you have ever watched a foundation of a house or building laid, you will notice that there are several elements to it. It is not just concrete. Metal bracing or wood forms are set in place first. Steel rebar goes in next, and bricks are used on the outside to pretty it up. The point here is that the foundation of a financial house may have any number of elements, all of which serve to insure, guarantee and make permanent the financial base.

Depending on your situation, life insurance can be one of those elements. Reasons why IUL qualifies for consideration in this regard are as follows:

Guaranteed principal AND guaranteed gains: Designed with a built-in ratchet/reset feature, IUL policies participate in stock market growth and lock in their principal and gains in a falling market. This feature was put to the test in 2008. As the stock market crashed around them, IUL investors remained unscathed. They didn't lose any principal or gains.

Beneficiary's payment is tax free: The death benefit from your IUL policy is paid to your named beneficiary in tax-free dollars.

Cash flow for retirement is tax free: By making use of the low-interest loan provision, you can enjoy a systematic income that is free of federal, state, local and alternative minimum tax.

What, Why and How Long for IUL

IUL is not for everyone. It is a long-term investment that should be examined carefully by your advisor to make sure that it supports your overall wealth management strategy.

IULs have many moving parts. They are designed to be held for at least 10 or even 15 years. Sometimes IULs are used as "ladder" investments, with the intention of employing this foundational investment to serve as steady stream of income 15 or 20 years down the road. However, prior to investing, have your advisor explain the early surrender fees.

Understand that a lapse in an IUL policy can trigger a taxable event. Again, your PCP planner can explain the implications. The cost of the insurance in an IUL is fully disclosed, but it is important to understand how it will affect the net return on your cash value. In addition, the issuing companies can change the policy rates and fees annually.

How Safe Are Insurance Products?

For some reason, most people that I've met tend to believe that banks and their FDIC insurance are the hallmark standard for safety. But when you compare the safety of banks and insurance companies side by side, you will see insurance companies come off the winners, both in recent times and the past.

The safety and financial stability of insurance companies was underscored by a 2013 CIPR (Center for Insurance Policy and Research) study, "Study on the State of the Life Insurance Industry." The study found that during the 10 years of economic turmoil between 2002 and 2012, the life insurance industry "significantly outperformed the banking industry."

Historically, banks failed while insurance companies survived. The CIPR research concluded that only 20 out of 350 insurers (5.7 percent) went into receivership during the Great Depression. Of those that failed, virtually all of the policyholder claims were still honored by solvent reinsurers. In contrast, more than 4,000 state and national banks failed in 1933 at the height of the Great Depression, and depositors lost about $1.3 billion.

Why are insurance companies historically safer? The law requires insurance companies to maintain reserves equivalent to 100 percent of their liabilities and the government regulates how those reserves are invested. So sure, there are no absolute guarantees in life. But as an industry, insurance companies have been able to provide a strong foundation for retirement investing.

CHAPTER EIGHT

The PCP Approach

"To be a star, you must shine your own light, follow your own path, and don't worry about the darkness, for that is when the stars shine brightest." – Napoleon Hill

In 1999, I took my business in an entirely new direction. It was obvious that the way I'd been trained — the way typical brokers and investment advisors approach investing — was not optimal for my clients. The old-school approach of "buy and hold" went counter to my intuition to know the "what, why and how long" of investing. So I tossed the outdated approach right out the window. Next, I ripped off the blinders that had been keeping me so intently focused on the stock market that I couldn't see the potential of non-market investments. Lastly, I stopped thinking about products and started thinking about a new process.

Initially, I didn't know what my new approach would look like. I didn't see anything out there that I wanted to imitate. So I put it on the back burner and let it stew. Occasionally, memories from my previous career in the medical field came to mind at the exact moment when I was trying to define my new investing approach.

One day, Kathie and I were reminiscing about some of the close calls — near deaths — she had witnessed as an emergency room nurse. If these patients' symptoms were lung or heart-related, I would often see these very same patients for diagnostic tests.

A middle-aged man came in with chest pains one day. That's not all that unusual in a hospital emergency room. Kathie realized that his symptoms could have had any number of causes. However, after some questioning, it became clear that the man had contracted strep throat a few months earlier. The man was generally healthy. He didn't have a primary care physician. When he got sick he just went to the nearest urgent care clinic. He was one of those people who wanted to avoid seeing a doctor if at all possible. The doctor on call quickly ascertained that the patient had nothing seriously wrong with him other than strep throat, which could be treated with antibiotics.

As the doc wrote the prescription for the antibiotics, he wrote a brief, one-line reminder that he customarily put on all prescriptions for antibiotics: "Be sure to take all of your medicine." Happy to be out of the doctor's office in record time, the man immediately went to the pharmacy and filled his prescription. He took his first dose and within 24 hours he was already feeling relief. The problem started on the fifth day, when the man forgot to take his medicine. His throat was no longer hurting and he simply forgot. Over the next few days, he did take a couple of his antibiotics — when he remembered — but then he stopped before he had finished his entire prescription. He reasoned that he'd given his immune system a jumpstart and now he would let his own body finish the healing process. He figured that, in this way, his body would actually come out of this battle stronger and more prepared for the next virus or infection.

Oh how wrong he was! Instead of going away, the infection quietly migrated to his heart. And though this doesn't happen often, it happens enough to be written up in the medical journals. By the time I saw this man, his heart valves had been permanently damaged. He was experiencing chest pains due to restricted blood flow. Fortunately, the man did not die, but he now has a lifelong heart condition that will need careful monitoring.

Why had all of this happened? You could argue that the man's problems began on the fifth day when he stopped taking his medicine. But in my mind, and in Kathie's mind, the real problem began when the man failed to entrust his health care to a primary care physician. Had the man gone to the same doctor on a regular basis, the case would have had a far different outcome. Had he consulted his primary care physician when he first noticed the beginnings of a sore throat, the doctor might have discovered the white spots on the back of his throat, diagnosed the problem earlier, prescribed the antibiotic earlier and nipped the problem in the bud.

As it turns out, the man had a mitral valve prolapse (MVP), or leaky heart valve — a condition he had had since birth. A long-term relationship with a doctor would have addressed this early. By itself, MVP is rarely a life-threatening condition. Most people with it have a normal life expectancy and often don't experience any symptoms. In fact, my mother had MVP after eight births and was sure she was going to die in her 60s. (She died at 98.) But, MVP patients are at higher risk for endocarditis, or infection of the heart tissue. For these patients, completing the entire round of antibiotics is an absolute must. Unfortunately, in this case, it made the difference between a short-term throat infection and a long-term heart condition.

In 1999, I adopted the **Primary Care Physician**, or **PCP approach,** to my financial advisory profession. If he had utilized a PCP approach, our man with the heart condition would have experienced constant care from a doctor who knew and understood his physical condition. Each doctor-patient conversation would have been an opportunity for a checkup. The patient would know the doctor and the doctor would know the patient. A reminder to "be sure to take all your medicine" would be understood, appreciated and complied with. Just as a PCP would take the time to understand a patient's health condition, a PCP financial advisor will take the time to understand a client's "wealth condition," so to speak, focusing on the long term, and referring his client to specialists if necessary to coordinate a treatment plan. Here is a snapshot of what my financial advisory practice looks like before and after the PCP adjustment.

PRE
VS.
POST

ADVISOR A	ADVISOR B
TYPICAL BROKER/INVESTMENT ADVISOR	FINANCIAL ADVISOR (WEALTH, TAX AND ESTATE)
STATIC MANAGEMENT BUY AND HOLD	BALANCED APPROACH/ COORDINATED PROCESS
SELLS PRODUCTS AND/OR MANAGEMENT CONTRACTS	UTILIZES ALL FINANCIAL TOOLS TO REDUCE, TRANSFER AND MANAGE RISKS
TRAINED TO PROMOTE $$ IN THE MARKET	

Right away, this new approach felt better to me and to my clients. It forced me to the do the thing that I'd wanted to do all along — build a closer and more trusting, long-term relationship with each client. It was as if a lightbulb lit up. Under the old model, I found myself drifting further and further from my clients. It reminded me of the problem I had at the hospital, when I moved from patient care to administration. Sure, my job as an administrator was important, but I longed for the closer relationships with the patients. Likewise, my practice had drifted more and more toward the shores of administration. Now, with the PCP approach, I was back to where I wanted to be. I was in a long-term, trusting relationship with my clients, helping them to heal from financial wounds and to plan for long-term success in retirement.

As of this writing, that change of approach happened 15 years ago, and I have witnessed a huge difference in the outcome for my clients. Now, when a client wants to pull money out of his tax-deferred retirement account for a new car or a special anniversary vacation, I can look him in the eye and tell him to first use money that is already exposed to taxes.

I'm not sure why, but this seems to be counterintuitive for some people. They think, "Most of my money is in my retirement account, so that is where I need to pull from when I have an unusual expense." But that is not a healthy decision from a tax standpoint. Within a few minutes, I can prove to him that it is costing him more — because he has to pay Uncle Sam his share — than if he were to take the money out of the liquid funds that we set up for this very purpose.

I have to laugh, because on the other hand, some people want to keep saving their emergency funds or contingency funds even when the very thing we saved the money for has finally presented itself! This is where having a skilled PCP can help. Your doctor can look you in the eyes and speak frankly to you. You know he or she has your best interest at heart. Likewise, the PCP financial advisor can look you in the eyes and help you separate an emotional decision from a sound financial decision. When I do this, my clients listen and later thank me.

To a large degree, I think that people have trouble making their financial decisions in the right order or at the best time simply because they are not used to making these types of decisions. So the advantage of working with a PCP who sees the outcomes of thousands of investing decisions over his lifetime and who also has some skin in the game, is that he is comfortable and has a long-term perspective on these seemingly tough choices.

I created a visual PCP model so that you can see exactly what the PCP financial advisor approach looks like. In the remainder of this book, we will go through each aspect of the model so that you can see how this all fits together to provide a holistic approach to your financial health.

PRIMARY CARE PHYSICIAN (PCP) COORDINATED APPROACH PLANNING

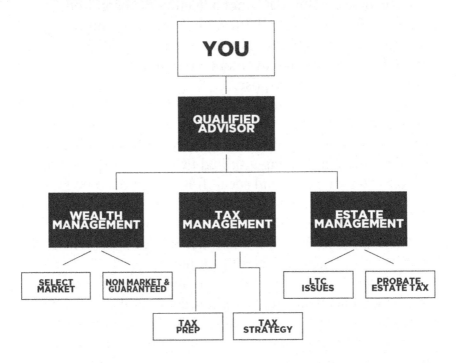

Smack dab at the top of this model is YOU. Not your money, not your investments not your tax returns. Just you. Your PCP wants to come to know what makes you unique. Your PCP wants to hear some of your stories, your history, your goals, dreams and aspirations. Your PCP wants to know you. Then, and only then, does your PCP want to see how your current choices are supporting your plans for the future.

Some financial advisors are stockbrokers with only securities licenses; others are licensed to sell insurance products. Some combine the two disciplines. Then there are those who have found a plan that works for most people, in their opinion — a cookie-cutter method. There are still other financial advisors who strive to keep up with the ever-changing financial landscape and the ever-changing needs of their clients.

If you've read this far, then you know that I am a constant learner, as attested to by my MBA and three other degrees. That all happened *before* I entered the financial profession. Even though I haven't added another "degree" to my list in the formal sense of the word, I have spent more time in seminars, with experts, and doing personal research in the financial profession than I spent in all of my years in college. Why? I'm not just in this to help you. I, too, have hopes, dreams, aspirations and plans for retirement. So we are all in this together. I'm learning and staying abreast of this ever-changing world to help you, but I'm also in it to help me. And to keep myself honest, I invest for me the same way that I invest for my clients. I'm totally transparent. I have skin in the game.

But guess what? Way too many investment advisors don't have skin in the game. A sobering 2009 study released by Morningstar tracked more than 4,300 mutual funds, and found that 51 percent of the managers owned *no shares* of the funds they managed. Hard to believe, isn't it? The remaining 49 percent of these mutual fund managers owned only token amounts of the mutual funds they managed.

This reminds me of the proverbial chef who won't eat his own cooking. I mean, can you imagine that? All the best chefs that I know can hardly keep their spoons out of their soup. They take a taste and then audibly purr, "mm-mm-mmm"… sometimes it needs just a pinch more of this or that. Or, maybe they pucker — it's a tad too tart — and then add a tablespoon of sugar or a dollop of sour cream.

In fact, I sometimes enjoy watching an occasional cooking show just to see how much pleasure the cooks take in their craft. The best chefs use all five senses when they are cooking. In one show, featuring Indian cuisine, I watched the chef demonstrate tadka, or "tempering." First, she visually examined the fresh curry leaves and chose only the best. Then, she rolled them in her hands and breathed in the pungent aroma. Clearly, this delighted her. Next, she dropped the herbs into a pan of hot oil, while making sure that the viewers could hear the telltale crackling as the oil pulled every drop of flavor from the herbs. As she cupped her hands and waved the ascending aroma to her face, I could almost smell the fresh curry leaves and garlic through my TV. But she wasn't done yet. This chef was not finished until she'd completed her dish, tasted it, and made me want to taste it too!

Now that is the kind of chef that I want to be cooking for me. What about you? Ask your advisor: Do you eat your own cooking? Do you have your money invested in all the same investments that you are recommending for me? You should get an honest and immediate answer if they have skin in the game.

The other beauty of the PCP approach is that by its nature, it lends itself to coordinated care. Again, let me use the medical model to illustrate the importance of coordinated care. It's actually pretty interesting, because we can trace medical trends from the 1800s, through the 1900s, and now into the 2000s and see that we've made a giant circle. We have come back to what works! The financial profession is just a little behind in figuring this out!

In the 1800s, a family would rely on their primary care physician, because really they had no other choice. Most towns felt very fortunate to have their own doctor and few had the luxury of two or more. So the family counted on their PCP to bring their babies into the world, to care for them during their flus and fevers, to set the occasional broken bones, to comfort the dying, and to guide them through the grief process.

Their PCP was also someone they saw at church and on the streets as they walked to school or to the local markets. The doctor knew the people and the people knew the doctor. There was a trust — a genuine relationship — and the PCP was the focal point through which all their other medical care was coordinated. If a little boy in the family needed special care or hospitalization, the trusted family PCP coordinated it, monitored it, and followed up. In this way, everyone on the PCP's "health team" knew that he knew the history of the patient and would ensure that everyone was working together for the best interest of the patient.

This continued all the way to World War II. At this point, America took its medical profession in a new direction, while Europe continued to focus on the PCP model. In America, people became convinced that specialization was a better way to go. So many people began sidestepping the primary care physician approach. Instead, they went to a heart specialist for their heart problems, a gastroenterologist for their digestive ailments, and so on.

In time, the shortcomings of this approach became all too apparent. One of the main risks of leaving the PCP model is adverse drug interaction. It's so common that you'd have to have spent the last 20 years living in a vacuum to miss all the warnings about it. Adverse drug interaction often happens when each specialist is prescribing medication in line with his or her specialty but not in coordination with the patient's other doctors.

For instance, according to the U.S. Food and Drug Administration's website, www.fda.gov, if a patient is prescribed Cordarone by his or her heart doctor to correct abnormal rhythms, and is also taking Zocor in doses higher than 20 mg for his or her cholesterol by another doctor, he or she is at risk for kidney failure or even death.

The risk for adverse drug interaction increases for patients on four or more medications. That accounts for about 40 percent of the population, according to the FDA site. But a risk that I found even more surprising was found in a Scientific American article titled, "How Primary Care Heals Healthy Disparities." The article said, "Among wealthier people, a big, perhaps surprising benefit of *primary care* (italics mine) is that it keeps patients from going too often to a specialist, where he can be overtreated or misdiagnosed."

The article later goes on to state, "Every test, every diagnostic procedure, every surgery has its own complication rates. For example, undergoing cardiac catheterization to see if the arteries in your heart are blocked slightly increases the risk of fatal internal bleeding — which is why you have to lie so still after the procedure." Unfortunately, I've seen too many people who died after a questionable, if not unnecessary, diagnostic procedure that may have been declined if the patient had a PCP coordinating his or her care.

As much as I hate to admit it, I've seen the same "over-doctoring" in the financial profession. Instead of operating under a coordinated plan, some of my clients come to me with three or four different advisors "prescribing" conflicting investments. This creates two major problems. First, although my prospective clients may have been experts in their own field, if they were honest with themselves they would have to admit they hadn't really evaluated whether their current advisors were very learned in their field of finance. Of course, all of their advisors were nice people. I understand that you don't do business with people you don't like, but being likeable doesn't necessarily make your advice credible.

Secondly, if a prospective client has three or four advisors, insurance agents, accountants, etc., it is rare that these advisors know each other or talk with each other. This lack of communication often results in things falling through the cracks. That's why we came up with the primary care physician (PCP) approach to money: a coordinated team of advisors, security representatives, tax accountants, tax planners and attorneys all working together for the benefit of our joint client.

CHAPTER NINE

Tax Management

"Thinking will not overcome fear but action will." – W. Clement Stone

Over the years, I've found that most people don't really pay attention to their tax returns. They view tax preparation as an annual duty that they quickly pawn off on their accountants. But instead of seeing their accountants as part of their team — professionals who can help them genuinely understand what they owe and why they owe it — most clients show up just long enough to write the check. This leaves the clients completely unaware of all of their options to keep more of their money in their pockets and out of Uncle Sam's.

Now, I'm not blaming it all on the clients. Many clients have accountants who believe that their role is to use the provided 1099s, W-2s or K-1s to file completed forms with the appropriate local, state and federal agencies. Job done. And to a large degree, they are right. But, if a client is only having tax preparation done, then the client is paying for someone to look back at the year's earnings. With the PCP approach, we take it one step further. We take recent tax returns and look forward to create a plan of action and reduce the amount of taxes owed in the future. In two words, we call this tax strategy. Together, tax preparation and tax strategy equals tax management.

With the PCP approach, past tax returns are critical. In fact, aside from getting to know you personally, getting to know and understand your tax returns is the next most important step.

Before I even glance at a client's investments, I do a comprehensive review and analysis of recent tax returns. Then I put my "what if" gear in motion. What if…what if…what if? What's interesting with tax returns is to do a side-by-side comparison. I'll lay the actual return beside a modified return reflecting a possible tax strategy. Trust me, no one wants to pay one penny more than his or her fair share of taxes. And when people see the difference, they become believers in proactive tax management.

Common "what if" questions include the following: What if I were to maximize all of my IRA-type contributions? What if I moved some of my funds currently exposed to taxes to tax-deferred investments? A not-so-common "what if" question involves tax-loss harvesting. Tax-loss harvesting occurs when you strategically sell depreciated assets to offset capital gains elsewhere in your portfolio. This is an especially good strategy if the depreciated assets no longer fit your investment objectives, such as when you are transitioning from your role as a wage earner to a retiree. Timing the sale of securities to offset capital gains saves tax dollars. If your capital losses exceed your gains, you can use up to $3,000 of your excess losses to offset ordinary income and carry any additional losses forward to offset capital gains or ordinary income in future years.

What if, instead of giving a cash donation to your favorite charity, you had given a highly appreciated asset that you'd owned for at least one year? It's a win-win for you and the charity. The charity will receive a higher donation because you won't have to deduct your long-term capital gains tax from the proceeds. At the same time, you get to claim the current fair market value (the appreciated value) as a tax deduction. In essence, the long-term capital gains tax that you would typically pay to Uncle Sam is instead paid as a gift to your favorite charity. If, however, the asset is at a loss, it is usually advantageous to sell the asset, claim the loss for tax purposes, and then donate the proceeds to your charity.

Now all of this forward thinking would be a lot easier if the tax law stayed static. But it doesn't. Tax laws are changing constantly. Just to give you an example, let's look at what has happened just since 2013.

In 2013, the new top marginal tax rate jumped from 35 percent to 39.6 percent on income above $400,000 (single filers) and $450,000 (married filing jointly). This same group was hit with a new 20 percent tax rate (up from 15 percent) on capital gains and qualified dividends. This new tax structure is screaming for people to wake up and implement strategic tax planning.

On top of that, the Affordable Care Act (a.k.a. Obamacare) went into effect in 2013. This means that taxpayers with modified adjusted gross income (MAGI) above $200,000 (single filers) and $250,000 (married filing jointly) may be liable for an additional 0.9 percent Medicare tax on income if they exceed the threshold and a Medicare surtax of 3.8 percent depending on their net investment income versus their MAGI.

Legitimate tax avoidance is best. But, next to that, tax credits — which come right off the bottom line that you owe Uncle Sam — are the next best thing. Up until the recently, we were rewarded for conserving energy and living green. However, many of these tax credits expired in 2013, including the non-business energy property credit. Homeowners were eligible to claim 10 percent of the purchase price of qualified energy-efficient products when they were installed at the taxpayer's main residence. Qualified products included:

- Advanced main air circulating fans.
- Central air conditioners.
- Exterior doors.
- Exterior windows and skylights.
- Furnaces.
- Heat pumps.

- Hot water boilers.

- Insulation.

- Metal or asphalt roofs with pigmented coatings or cooling granules designed to reduce heat gain.

- Water heaters.

Even though this tax credit is temporarily gone, I believe that we will see it again. But most people aren't paying careful attention. After all, it's hard enough to juggle everything in your own profession, let alone keep up with the never-ending tax law changes.

But not all the energy credits have expired. The Federal Tax Credits for Consumer Energy Efficiency remain intact through 2016. These can be pretty significant, and unlike the non-business energy tax credit already mentioned, these credits apply to products installed in your main residence *and* your secondary residence. Unfortunately, it does not apply to your rental property.

One of my favorite products is the geothermal heat pump (GHP). I'm fascinated by the science of this product because it rewards the investor in several ways. First, it significantly reduces your heating and cooling costs. Let's face it, many things are in life are optional, but energy to run our homes is not. And I don't know anyone who is predicting that energy costs are going down. So if you can invest now in a system that will stabilize your future heating and cooling costs, that has to add to your retirement security.

Secondly, the federal government is going to subsidize your upfront investment with generous tax credits through 2016. You can go to www.energystar.gov to get the tax credit specifications. But to put it concisely, the tax credit is 30 percent of the cost with no upper limit for systems placed in service by Dec. 31, 2016.

Thirdly, the older I get the more I love this earth that I live on. Like so many boomers, I want to leave this planet in the best shape possible for future generations. GHPs leave a dramatically reduced carbon footprint when compared to oil, natural gas, propane or electricity.

Everything that I'd managed to dig up on the subject was confirmed when I was reading the investment section of Forbes from Feb. 28, 2014. I ran across the article, "How Geothermal Heat Pumps Can Soar Like Solar." Author Tom Konrad said, "They (GHPs) do the job of heating and cooling a building more efficiently than any other option. Despite the larger upfront cost, they are a mature technology and usually the most economic option for buildings that can accommodate them." According to his research, GHPs can reduce your heating and cooling costs by up to 80 percent. To me, saving money is even better than earning money! The federal government's generous tax credit just sweetens the pie.

Now why did I take you on this tangent? I think responsible PCP advisors always have their eyes and ears opened. By keeping up with tax credits, tax changes, energy costs, and even global markets, I'm in a better position to coordinate your "wealth care." So all of this fascinating information on GHPs gives you a little glimpse into how my mind works. I'm constantly on the lookout for ways to save, preempt cost increases, anticipate changes and stay ahead of the curve.

By the way, before we leave the topic of Federal Tax Credits for Consumer Energy Efficiency — take a peek at the solar energy systems, which include solar water heating and photovoltaic systems, residential small wind energy systems and residential fuel cells (tax credits only allowed on principal residence). These energy efficiency products are not for everyone, maybe they are not even for most people. But don't throw the idea out the window before you give it a second look.

This brings us back to the importance of having skin in the game. Sure, every investment advisor files taxes. But is the advisor doggedly determined to be paying the least amount of tax as possible? Are they stubbornly asking the "what if" questions on their own taxes and running side-by-side comparisons? When an advisor is doing this for his own return, he is more likely to know what questions to ask about your return. If your advisor is not asking you questions about your past tax returns and running comparisons, then your advisor is not using the PCP approach.

I will tell you this: it's a rare case when I cannot find at least one way to improve on someone's tax liability. Sometimes my find is minor, but sometimes it's rather shocking. One of the most upsetting cases to me was when I found a man who had been advised to invest all the money in his IRA into tax-free municipal bonds. He had been erroneously told that his future IRA distributions would come out tax-free. News flash: Anything that goes into a traditional IRA will be taxed when it comes out no matter what it is invested in. Also, this lopsided investment went against the old rule of diversification: "Don't put all your eggs in one basket." When interest rates go up, bond values go down. It is unwise to make an investment for the sole purpose of saving taxes. If the investment does not make sense based on its own merits, it is usually not the best choice.

It's also important for you to know that, as motivated as I am to stay current with tax and investing strategies, I know can't do it alone. And as I've mentioned several times in this book, it's important to know what you don't know. That is why I have a team of tax accountants, tax planners and attorneys all working together for the benefit of each client. That is the PCP approach, coordinated care by professionals who all know each other and work as a team. That's the approach that you deserve as you plan and enjoy your retirement.

CHAPTER TEN

Digging Deeper with Foundational Investments

"Always do what you are afraid to do." – Ralph Waldo Emerson

Researchers at Stanford University used age progression software to show people how they would look when they got older as part of an experiment to determine whether such awareness would affect their saving and investment habits. Their conclusion, published in the Journal of Marketing Research in 2011, indicated when people saw themselves growing older it reinforced the need to allocate more money to their retirement accounts.

I have seen this software. A beautiful young woman's face appears on the screen of the monitor. As the seconds tick by, her face develops fine lines around her eyes, then her mouth. Her hair gradually turns from black to gray. The lines become wrinkles and her once youthful face becomes the face of first a mature woman in her 40s and then progresses to that of an older woman in her 80s and finally as a 100-year-old. To reinforce the message that the user will get old one day, the app then flickers back and forth between the current photo and the aged photo.

In the experiment, 50 people were shown an aged photo of themselves and asked to allocate a hypothetical $1,000 among four choices: a checking account, a fun vacation, a retirement fund, or buying a present for someone special. The same question was posed to another group after viewing a current photo of themselves. Who do you think chunked more money into the savings account? The ones who saw the aged picture of themselves saved twice as much as the others — hypothetically, of course.

But how we see ourselves in retirement makes a difference in how we invest. If we put our retirement portfolio into an aging software, would we see it increasing in size, shrinking in size, disappearing entirely or staying the same? Decisions we make when we are approaching retirement can make the difference. Laying a foundation of solid, wind-resistant materials may not be all that exciting, but trust me; your older self is going to love the predictable, steady, no-surprises paychecks that will be the result of the decisions made by your younger self.

According to the Ernst & Young study, "The Likelihood of Outliving Their Assets," your older self may be living a whole lot longer than you expected. The average life expectancy is typically listed as 85 for males and 88 for females. But you can't just go with a single average life expectancy. Why? Because your *actual* life expectancy is determined on the age you have *attained.* In other words, the longer you live, the longer you will live. Here is information gleaned from a chart that appears on the Social Security website.

MALE VS. FEMALE

MALE (58)		FEMALE (58)	
AGE REACHED	EXPECTANCY	AGE REACHED	EXPECTANCY
58	83	58	85
62	84	62	86
66	85	66	87
70	86	70	88

According to the government website, about one out of every four 65-year-olds today will live past age 90, and one out of 10 will live past age 95. The Ernst & Young study found that six out of 10 middle-class new retirees were on track to outlive their financial assets UNLESS they reduced their standard of living by 24 percent. The study defines "middle-class" as those with pre-retirement annual incomes of $50,000, $75,000, or $100,000. Even more unsettling was the study's finding that 75 percent with seven years to go before their retirement were projected to outlive their assets if they didn't reduce their standard of living. All of this isn't to scare you, but to endear you to your future older self.

Share some of your current earning with him or her now, and you will be happier in the future. The Ernst & Young study assumes that you are receiving Social Security benefits and that your income needs in retirement will be only 65 to 75 percent of your pre-retirement income because you no longer have expenses related to employment. The first group in the study has the advantage of a defined benefit pension plan. Thanks to their employer, regular retirement paychecks will be coming in the mailbox right alongside their Social Security checks. Just for the record, as this is written, only 33 percent of retirees have a defined benefit plan, and that percentage will shrink dramatically the future.

More Ernst & Young findings: A married couple aged 58 currently earning $50,000 a year has a 53 percent chance of outliving their financial assets. However, if they are willing to reduce their standard of living today by 23 percent, and then put that money into retirement savings, they can reduce that risk to a mere 5 percent. Now you might think that the picture looks a lot brighter for couples making $100,000 a year, but that is not the case. A 58-year-old couple with a defined benefit pension plan and annual earnings of $100,000 a year has a 51 percent risk of outliving their assets and will need to reduce their standard of living by 25 percent to reduce their risk of outliving their assets to 5 percent. A 58-year-old couple who earns $50,000 annually but without the advantage of a defined-benefit pension plan has a 94 percent chance of outliving their assets unless they reduce their standard of living now by 46 percent and sock the savings produced by such a move into foundational investments.

We could go on, but you should get the picture: If you are the average Joe or Jane, you may want to consider paring back your lifestyle, saving more money, and building that solid financial foundation we have been talking about — the sooner the better.

The Danger of Playing Catch-Up

Some who fear they are behind in their retirement goals may reason that one way to play catch-up is to take on more risk. That's like doubling down at the gambling tables in Las Vegas. The house may love it, but for you it's a long shot you can't afford to take. The Ernst & Young study I've discussed so far concludes with this bit of sage advice: "Without additional guaranteed lifetime income streams, such as income provided by an annuity, middle income Americans are at high risk of outliving their financial assets and living their final years in poverty."

Ernst & Young doesn't specify what type of annuity it recommends, but I suggest you consider the hybrid annuity for one main reason: The income guarantee it provides. Fixed index annuities with optional income riders are relative newcomers to the annuity scene and they have apparently captured the attention of millions of Americans who are nearing or in retirement. In a study released March 13, 2014, Sheryl J. Moore, president and CEO of both Moore Market Intelligence and Wink, Inc., noted about annuities: "This was the fifth consecutive record-setting year at $36.8 billion, topping last year's record of $8.5 billion by 13.4 percent. Indexed annuities continue to gain more acceptance as rates on traditional fixed money instruments remain low and consumers seek-out the guarantees that are inherent in indexed annuities."

CHAPTER ELEVEN

The Walls and Windows of Your Financial House

"You block your dream when you allow your fear to grow bigger than your faith." – Mary Manin Morrissey

A wise old man once told me, "Don't treat your home like an investment." I was young at the time. He was suggesting that I should create a home that our family would love to live in — rather than thinking only of its future resale value. In reality, both are important. I would never want to overbuild for an area, but at the same time, if I can't enjoy my home and have it reflect my family's personality, then I have to ask myself: Is it really *my* home?

I believe that the same principle applies to building your financial house. Imagine if you walked into five houses and they all had the same floor plan, the same carpet selection, the same pictures on the walls, and the same china in the cupboard! It would be very unsettling. You'd begin to ask: Who are these people and why are they living this way? Did someone tell them that this is the ***best*** way or the ***only*** way to design a house?

In retirement planning, foundational investments may have similar characteristics in the respect that they are safe and principal is guaranteed. But the main living space of the financial house lends itself to personalization. If it is not, then most likely an old-school advisor who is not using the PCP approach is the one constructing it. Just like your personal residence should reflect your individuality, your unique circumstances, goals and preferences will dictate what goes on the "walls" of your financial house. The personal care physician advisor takes the time to know your financial makeup, just the way a private physician knows your physical makeup, and gears your investments to suit your needs, preferences and personality.

For example, a portfolio in your retirement years should probably include **select market** investments. What does that mean? Well, for some investors, this means a conservative stock selection and maybe even some bonds. For others it may mean more adventuresome investments, such as new markets, commodities or currencies. Just because you retire doesn't mean that you have to stop having fun. If you are a do-it-yourself investor, the type who likes invest in the market and watch the ticker symbols on your personal computer, then there should be a place for that in your planning. The only thing that really changes is the percentage of money that you place in these investments. After all, if it is a working retirement plan, you are still insistent on diversity and growth with safety.

But regardless of the variety of market investments that you prefer, in most cases, you will be best served by investing in an exchange-traded fund (ETF) and closed-end funds because both give you maximum speed to trade anytime during market hours — something not possible with mutual funds.

Exchange Traded Funds (ETFs)

Necessity is the mother of invention, and that pretty much sums up how ETFs came into existence. Back in the late 1970s, people began to notice that the major market indices were repeatedly outperforming actively managed portfolio funds. Doing the math, it didn't take a genius to realize that there was more money to be made by investing in an indexed fund than having a managed portfolio. However, regulations had to catch up with research, and it wasn't until 1993 that the first ETF, the SPDR S&P 500 ETF, was launched.

Initially, institutional investors used ETFs to hedge and manage their cash. However, because these index funds trade as any other common stock on the market — hence the name exchange-traded funds — they have become more popular for individual investors. By 2008, ETF assets had grown to $94 billion, which was distributed among 231 sector and commodities ETFs. By 2014, there were more than 1,500 ETFs managing more than $1.7 trillion in assets.

The first closed-end funds (funds that trade like any other stock) appeared in the U.S. in the late 1800s. Just to show you how quickly ETFs have caught on, let us compare this to traditional mutual funds. The first mutual fund in the U.S. was created in 1924. However, it wasn't until the 1980s — 60 years later — that mutual funds gained widespread acceptance. So the 21-year track record of ETFs is nothing short of amazing. Or is it? Actually, an ETF is a mutual fund with a couple of tweaks that give it five clear advantages. But let's first look at its similarity to a traditional mutual fund.

Similarities to Mutual Funds

One of the most attractive features of mutual funds is that they offer diversity for even small investors. Mutual funds give you the opportunity to invest in Blue Chip stocks, municipal bonds, gold, foreign currency, junk bonds, growth stocks or countless other assets while spreading the risk by owning shares in a diversified portfolio. Additionally, mutual funds have a pre-determined structure; they are managed and regulated. These are the points in common for traditional mutual funds share and ETFs.

ETF and Closed-End Fund Advantages

Intraday trading: Today, more than ever, timing is everything. In a traditional mutual fund, if you decide that you want to redeem your shares at 10 in the morning, you can place your order, but it won't be filled until after 4 p.m. Eastern

Standard Time, when the stock exchange closes. Then all the orders to buy and sell are processed, so you lose the advantage of intraday trading. ETFs, on the other hand, trade just like a common stock. You simply call your broker and place your order. Liquidity is high because ETFs typically trade at considerably higher volumes than individual stocks. Historically, ETFs tend to hold very close to their net asset value, reducing expenses associate with trades.

Lower costs: Mutual funds are expensive to manage. When you purchase or redeem shares, you generate "paperwork" because funds must be tracked and properly credited. The fund manager must go into the market to buy or sell investments to satisfy your order and the fund manager charges fees. These higher administrative costs and management fees eat into your profits. Because they differ in structure, ETFs have considerably lower costs.

According to Dave Nadig, director of research at IndexUniverse, the average index equity mutual fund has an administrative cost of 1.46 percent, versus the corresponding ETF fund, which operates at an average cost of 0.53 percent. Many ETFs have administrative costs of only 0.09 percent to 0.40 percent. To a large degree, the savings are due to virtually no "paperwork," or tracking of individual investors since ETFs trades like stocks. Additionally, ETFs practice passive management, which saves investors expenses associated with active trading generally associated with mutual fund managers. All in all, ETFs have fewer costs to diminish your returns.

Tax efficiency: Mutual funds, by their very nature, try to outperform the market by actively trading investments. In fact, fund managers' earnings are often tied to reaching predetermined benchmarks. This active trading results in capital gains — sometimes to the tune of 23.5 percent according to researcher Nadig. Just to put this into perspective, if 23.5 percent of the gains are sacrificed to taxes, that can drive a 10 percent pre-tax return down to a 7.7 percent after-tax return.

By contrast, ETFs are designed to mirror the index and are therefore lend themselves to passive trading. According to Nadig's research, in 2008 less than 10 percent of ETFs paid capital gains and of the few that did, none paid more than 1 percent. You know how I feel about taxes. ETFs keep Uncle Sam's fingers a little further away from your pie.

Transparency: One of the biggest gripes about mutual funds is their lack transparency. While they do report their net asset value on a daily basis, most mutual funds only report their list of investment allocations quarterly. In other words, they don't tell you which stocks and how many of each stock is in the portfolio each day. More than once, mutual funds have gotten into trouble by deviating from their stated objectives. Often, the motivating factor was a fund manager's trying to nab a bigger paycheck by temporarily altering his asset allocation in an attempt to reach his benchmark.

Conversely, ETFs list their asset allocation daily on their websites. You can also track the net asset value (NAV) of any ETF to see whether the ETF is trading at its NAV. Historically, ETFs trade very close to their NAV, but sometime a large purchase or sell orders will temporarily tilt the value. This can help you determine the best time to buy or sell. In other words, ETFs give today's investors the kind of control that they want over their investments. ETFs give investors virtually "total transparency."

Easy access to many markets: As you can see, with reduced administrative cost and all the ease of trading on the stock market, ETFs are much lighter on their feet than mutual funds. Because of this, ETFs can be incredibly responsive to new trends and developing markets. ETFs cover every major market index including the S&P, the Dow Jones, the NASDAQ, global markets as well as industry-specific portfolios such as energy, health and technology. You may even invest in country-specific ETFs, such as Japan, China and the U.K.

ETFs may also be representative of regional, international and emerging markets, commodities, currencies and virtually all sectors of the equities market, including large caps, small caps and growth stocks. All of this is important to today's investors because we now live in a global economy. It's a bit egocentric to think that all the best investments are in our own backyard. The research is now as readily available as the opportunities. In my opinion, ETFs give us the best way — for the five reasons listed above — to make select market investments for optimal wealth management.

ETFs Are Not for Everyone

In an April 25, 2014 interview posted on ETF.com, Deborah Fuhr, partner and founder of London-based research company ETFGI, advised potential investors to ask themselves the following questions before investing in an ETF:

- What are your financial goals?

- Where do you want to invest?

- If you want exposure to U.S. markets, which benchmark best represents that exposure?

- Do you want something tilted or fundamental?

These questions are exactly in line with the PCP approach. I have some clients who have never owned a commodity in their lives. Commodities meet neither their needs nor their risk tolerances. Other clients do enjoy trading in commodities. They have specific funds set aside for their higher-risk investments and by careful management have "earned the right" to enjoy trading right on through retirement. When they invest in emerging stocks, foreign markets or global ETFs, they feel like they have skin in the game. They stay up to date with the daily global news and it keeps them tuned in to our quickly changing world.

By using ETFs, they not only get a pre-picked and diversified portfolio; they have the option to sell short or buy on margin. If you don't know what that is, don't do it! You could be playing with blasting caps, financially speaking. Granted, most of my retired clients aren't interested in this kind of hands-on trading, but for those who are, ETFs can be a hedge for inflation and add some growth potential to their wealth management plan. All of that is determined by your financial goals.

Regarding the rest of Fuhr's questions, imagine if every S&P index ETF was an exact mirror of the S&P 500. These are termed replicate index-based ETFs. The ETF holds every security in the given index and it invests in all the securities in the target index. But some index funds are tilted. Purposely, these ETFs hold only a sampling of the securities in the target index. Each fund then has a unique tilt. This is called a sample-based ETF, and it will perform differently from a replicate index-based ETF. These differences are all transparent, but I think it demonstrates the need to have a well-informed advisor to guide you with the PCP approach to select the most suitable ETF for your needs.

Fuhr also suggested that investors look at the total cost of ownership. In other words, as exchange traded securities, there are brokerage commissions to be paid when ETFs are bought and sold. It's not cost effective to do many small transactions, such as investing $50 a month, to accumulate shares over the long haul.

The majority of clients in the PCP approach do not use traditional commission trading. They prefer that their advisors have skin in the game. I've already mentioned the 2009 study released by Morningstar, which found that 51 percent of the managers owned no shares in the fund they manage. Of the remaining 49 percent, most own a token amount of their funds when compared to their compensation and net worth. Here's the final breakdown:

- 413 managers invested more than $1,000,000.

- 197 managers invested between $500,001 and $999,999.

- 679 managers invested between $100,001 and $500,000.

- 285 managers invested between $50,001 and $100,000.

- 393 managers invested between $10,001 and $50,000.

- 159 managers invested between $1 and $10,000.

More than half of all the fund managers in the study had less than $100,000 invested in their own funds. That's certainly not much skin in the game. As a client, you should want your market positions under a true actively managed portfolio — one in which your representative is also invested, using a combination of closed-end funds, ETFs, stocks and bonds. This way you know your representative is keeping a close eye on your market investments and making the same changes for everyone at the same time.

REITs and Other Non-Market Investments

I like to keep moving forward and do everything for a reason. With the rest of our financial house in place, it's time to take a closer look at REITs (Real Estate Investment Trusts) and other non-market investments. In earlier chapters, I mentioned their benefits briefly — they are non-correlated and add true diversity.

Though you may not have heard about REITs, they have actually been around for as long as many baby boomers! In 1960, Congress created REITs so that the average American could invest in income-producing real estate. Income-producing real estate includes the raw land and all the improvements on it, such as apartments, shopping malls, or hotels. Equity REITs invest in the actual properties and generate income from rent, while mortgage REITs invest in the mortgages of these properties and generate income from interest. Either way, when you invest in an REIT, you are always investing in a portfolio of diversified properties.

Benefits of REITs

Diversity: These non-correlated investments historically dampen the vicissitudes of your overall portfolio and serve as a

112

hedge against inflation. According to some estimates, nearly 50 million Americans are invested in REITs in 401(k)s alone.

Dividends: By definition, REITs pay out 90 percent of their taxable income to shareholder in the form of dividends. According to Money Magazine in April 2012, "REITs have delivered impressive long-term gains, with annualized returns of more than 10 percent for the past 10 years. And with dividend yields ranging from more than 3 percent to almost 8 percent in recent years, REITS have long been a go-to investment for retirees looking for reliable income." Dividends are taxable as ordinary income.

Performance: Some REITs are publicly traded and others are non-traded. According to REITWatch, a monthly report on the Real Estate Investment Trust Industry that tracks publicly traded REITs, equity REITs regularly outperform the Dow, the S&P 500 and the NASDAQ.

Transparency: REITs operate under the guidelines set in place by Congress. Publicly traded REITs and public non-listed REITs both file with the Security and Exchange Commission (SEC) and make regular disclosures including quarterly and annual financial reports.

Growth: Equity REITs returns, held for the long term, historically exceed the rate of inflation, helping investors preserve future buying power.

Equipment Leasing

We touched on equipment leasing earlier in the book. What is it exactly and how could you invest in it? It's obvious that FedEx and United Parcel Service operate thousands of trucks, but most of those are leased. Factories have changed with the times and lease much of their manufacturing equipment. The same goes for oil companies and other industries. Equipment leasing is a big business. There are several multi-billion dollar leasing programs out there and you can plug some of your money into them for a steady return.

The main reason for mentioning this is because it is a non-market investment. There is some risk involved and the success of the investment will likely ebb and flow with the general economy or, more particularly, the sector of the economy in where your investment placed. But it is not subject to the twitches and nervous tics of the stock market. I should caution you that equipment leasing is generally ***not*** appropriate for retirement accounts from a tax point of view. This investment is better suited for people who are making a lot of money and have done everything they can to manage their taxes. Other non-market investments include energy programs, business development programs and more.

The Non-PCP Approach

When I talk about non-market programs in my seminars I ask the audience, "How many people in this room know all about the investments I just covered?" Rarely does even a single hand shoot up. Non-market programs have been around for a long time but few know about them. Some brave soul in the audience will invariably ask, "Why don't other advisors tell people about these things?" I know why and you can probably guess why. Because it is so much easier for a broker to say, "John, give me all your money and I'll take care of you. I'm going to put it in this pie diagram with a whole bunch of mutual funds so that we're not investing all in one place. We're going to invest in large-cap, small-cap, medium-cap and government bonds."

To me, that's not being a professional. I know what a professional is. For me, professionalism is the PCP approach and putting the client first. It's getting to know each client and helping him or her build a portfolio as comfortable and as true to his or her specific needs and wants as possible. I have been a professional for many years, even before I came into this business. I want to sleep well at night knowing that I gave my clients the most suitable advice for them personally. That's important to me.

114

CHAPTER TWELVE

Putting the Roof on Your Financial House

"Live to the limit every minute of every day.
Do it! I say. Whatever you want to do, do it now!
There are only so many tomorrows."

– Michael Landon

The purpose of a roof is to protect everything under it. We seem to have no problem appreciating the value of the roof on our home. In fact, if we ever let our roof get into disrepair, we often see immediate negative results, such as dripping water that can ruin our ceilings, our walls, our floors or anything affected by the leak. But most people resist putting the roof — the protection — on their financial house.

The first layer of roofing is some type of long-term care (LTC) insurance. I know it may be expensive, but the statistics don't lie. According to the U.S. Department of Health and Human Services, someone turning 65 today has almost a 70 percent chance of needing some type of long-term care services and supports in their remaining years. Women need care for an average of 3.7 years and men, 2.2 years. One-third of today's 65 year-olds may never need long-term care support, but one-fifth will need it for longer than five years.

The average cost for five years in a skilled nursing home is $500,000. I know, I know. I can almost hear the groan from here. Plenty of other people feel the way you likely feel. In 2012, Northwestern Mutual surveyed 2,194 U.S. adults and found that:

- 80% felt that there is a greater need for long-term care now that people are living longer.

- 45% weren't sure how they plan to address their own potential long-term care needs.

- 67% believed that the cost of providing long-term care will rise faster than the return of their retirement savings.

- 53% believed that long-term care costs will double in the next 14 years.

- 28% were currently saving for future long-term care needs.

Coming from a medical background, I know the value of getting proper care when we are least able to care for ourselves. I also know why most people buck at buying long-term care insurance. It's the same reason that I resist it. The premiums are high and they can be raised at the discretion of the insurer. Moreover, we may never need the coverage and if that's the case, there is no refund. Those premiums are gone. It is like car insurance. If you don't need to use it, congratulations! Thank you for playing and have a nice day.

I looked up some statistics on the chances of using LTC compared with other types of insurance:

- Homeowner's insurance: You have a 1 in 88 chance of using it.

- Car insurance: You have a 1 in 44 chance of using it.

- **Long-term care insurance: You have a 2 in 5 chance of using it.**

I know. It surprised me too. So here are some options and some advice in case you are considering protecting your financial house with this layer of roofing:

Option I: Purchase traditional LTC insurance. If you do this, you should purchase it from a non-captive, independent agent and make sure he or she obtains bids from at least two or three A+ rated companies before you buy. Premiums vary and offerings vary from company to company. If you subscribe to the coordinated PCP approach to caring for your financial house as described in previous chapters, you want an agent who is works for **you** and is loyal to **you,** not some company.

What if you are no longer healthy enough to qualify for traditional LTC? What if you've "aged out," so to speak and the premiums are just too high? Or what if you simply want to consider other options. Well, keep reading.

Option II: Let's look at the "what ifs." What would happen if you were to set aside $100,000 just in case? What if you could invest that $100,000 with an insurance company, get it back any time you wanted it, but as long as it stays there it has a *multiplier.* It multiplies to $245,000 *in the event* you need long-term care and you could get the money to pay for the care out of the contract in a tax-free monthly check until the LTC benefit was exhausted.

ASSET PROTECTION

TAX-FREE
MONTHLY
LTC
BENEFIT

TAX-FREE
DEATH
BENEFIT

GUARANTEED

$245,694

IRA

MONEY
MARKET

$100,000

CD'S   ANNUITY

SAVINGS

OPTION A
LIQUID*

OPTION B
$100,000 STILL LIQUID

THIS ILLUSTRATION IS A HYPOTHETICAL AND
REPRESENTS A 60 YEAR OLD, NON-SMOKING FEMALE.

Now it's your turn to ask me the "what if" questions.

"What if I never need the LTC benefit? What if I am one of those fortunate few, who dies peacefully in my sleep?"

In that case, the higher value goes tax-free to your heirs.

"What if 10 years go by and I decide to use the money for something else. Can I still get it?"

Yes, but after four or five years go by you will get a whole lot more than the original $100,000. The insurance company would have to pay you interest to the tune of around 3 or 4 percent (this varies with the prevailing interest rate).

118

This option may not be perfect, but in my book it's better than buying a traditional LTC policy and paying high premiums that may increase at the discretion of the insurance company for care that you may never need.

Option III: Certain hybrid annuities available today have income riders with guaranteed growth. After you turn on the income, if you need long-term care, that income can double to help pay the costs. No underwriting is required, so your current age or state of health won't stand in your way. If you don't use any or all of the long-term care benefits the proceeds pass to your heirs.

While we are on the subject of insurance, make sure you have a knowledgeable agent check your life insurance. In reviewing life insurance for couples, I have found that 60 percent to 70 percent of the policies will expire before the people do. When in doubt, we suggest you do an "in-force policy illustration" directly from the home office of the company to see whether your premiums will increase and determine whether your cash value is decreasing or about to decrease. Find out whether your policy is guaranteed to last until you die. Can it be better without costing you more?

To Trust or Not to Trust

Another important layer of roofing is the living trust. Here's why. Most couples' ultimate retirement goal can be summed up in this one phrase: "A comfortable retirement with savings and investments which will outlast our lives so we can pass on our estate, in its entirety, to our loved ones."

There seems to be a lot of confusion about the subject today. Some say they have heard that the **federal** exclusion is $5.25 million and they don't need a trust anymore. First of all, the federal exclusion is a moving target that is difficult to plan around. I had to smile when I read that Congress passed legislation on Jan. 1, 2013, to make the 2012 exemption of $5 million "permanent." When Congress calls a law "permanent," that doesn't mean they couldn't change it again. Although there is little impetus to do that as this is written, it could happen.

What about **state** estate tax? Some states have exclusions and some exclude all. Do you know the exclusion in your state?

Then there is the question of probate. Some are advised that they do not have enough assets to need a trust. I would get a second opinion on that.

Others will say there will be no probate on their estate because they have a will. Actually, a will guarantees probate. A will is written to the courts. In a way, you are hiring the legal system to supervise the transfer of your estate, and of course, they need to be paid. There's certainly nothing wrong with that. But some choose to save that cost. They also choose to **immediately transfer** assets of their estate to their loved ones rather than subject them to the delays of the probate process.

Finally, some would prefer that their estate matters are kept private rather than exposed to the public. The probate process is a public record. With a will and the required probate, here is a list of who gets paid and in what order:

1. *Attorneys/creditors*

2. *Executor*

3. *Appraisers*

4. *Filing fees*

5. *Taxes*

6. *Your heirs*

There are several reasons to avoid probate:

- **Probate court costs.**

- **Attorney/administrative fees:** Those first two could easily add up to 6 percent or more of probatable assets.

- **Waiting periods:** It is not uncommon to wait one year or more.

120

- ***Public disclosure:*** In many cases, your neighbor can go to the courthouse, ask for the file and make copies right there of any assets that are being reviewed by the court.

- ***Outside third-person control:*** Once the process starts, the appointed executor has very little control.

My wife and I have a trust. This grants us peace of mind in knowing that if the plane goes down, my oldest daughter has immediate control to distribute our estate. She can do this without losing control of the process due to probate. She becomes the immediate trustee upon our death.

Not long ago, a lady came to me who had recently lost her husband and who had joint tenancy with him. Everything transferred to her just fine without probate — the house, farm and all bank and stock accounts. But she got this idea that since everything went so well with the joint tenancy with her husband that she would now become joint tenant with her son on everything. Because she didn't know what she didn't know, she created a few problems for herself.

Problem No. 1, if her son was in an accident that was deemed his fault and the other party sued for damages, joint tenancy opened the door to everything she owned. The second problem had to do with "step-up in value." Had she left everything in just her name, suffered the probate, or had a **living trust**, or a transfer on death (TOD)/payable on death (POD), all values of the estate upon her death would have been stepped up to market value and the son would be able to sell assets with no capital gains.

However, if the son received everything through joint tenancy, he would pay no probate but would have to share in the original cost basis of everything his mother owned. In other words, he would lose the "step up" benefit. There was a stock in the estate that had been purchased many years ago for $10,000 but was now worth $200,000. The tax on that one stock would have been enormous.

Here is another example of the failure of joint tenancy. *Title passes at the instant death occurs, which can cause problems when two people die in a common event.* Years ago, there was a couple in their second marriage. Each had children from a previous marriage. They decided to buy a new home together in joint tenancy. There was a fire in the home and they both died in the fire. Upon an investigation, they found the husband had died in the bed and the wife had died near the back door. The ruling was made that the husband had died first; therefore the house became the wife's. Because she died second, all the insurance proceeds from the house went just to her children. His children were left out. A trust could have prevented that disaster.

Lastly, there was a couple who had seven children. They owned a cabin in the northern woods. They had owned and enjoyed it for many years and wanted to always keep it in the family. They got this idea that they would put all their kids as joint tenants. That way, in their mind, it would always be there for the children even after the parents died. That may sound logical, but here is the rest of the story: As time rolled on, their kids all moved away to different states and the parents fell on some hard times. They needed money.

Many years had passed and the children had never shown any interest in the cabin, so they decided to sell it. Making the children joint tenants was quite easy, but as they found out, removing them was much harder. Each one of the seven had to sign off. That was bad enough, but all seven were now married and the law required that all the spouses had to sign off as well. As you might have guessed, some did not desire to do so. Once again, the privacy of a trust could have eliminated this problem.

Obviously, it is always better to have help from a knowledgeable professional.

Fortunately, when my mother was diagnosed with Alzheimer's disease, we had a trust for her. Without the trust, which included a durable power of attorney, we would have had to file with the court for guardianship and for the duration of her life, we would have had to report to the court annually and pay the cost associated with it. All that was avoided because we were proactive with a trust.

122

In summary, the benefits of a trust include:

- No probate.

- Ease of administration: Change it any time you want.

- Protection of children and other beneficiaries: Shares for someone declared incompetent or a person on government assistance can be protected.

- Creditor, spousal and spendthrift protections: While living, assets are much harder to attack while registered in a trust. At death, wills are easily contested because they are public; trusts are not because they are private.

- All estate assets governed by one plan.

- Avoidance of joint property problems.

- Possible income tax and estate tax savings.

- Non-resident trustees can serve: Not always true for executors of a will.

- Trust easily moved to another state: Trusts are legal in all 50 states.

- "Ancillary" probate avoided for assets in other states: Those with properties in multiple states won't have to worry about multiple probates to bring everything back to their resident state for final probate.

- Privacy.

- Reduces risk of contest.

Unfortunately, not all attorneys really know trusts and trust planning. Most of them will freely tell you if they are not knowledgeable in this area. My son-in-law is a good example. Although he is an attorney and graduated at the top of his class in law school, he needed to come to our firm to learn about trusts and estate planning. Do your homework and work with a competent and knowledgeable advisor who can connect you with the right attorney.

What About Your Advisor?

Does he or she know taxes, tax planning, trusts and estate planning? For most people, if their portfolio is making money, they are happy. If it is losing money, they are not happy. But there is so much more to successful financial planning than that. Start today to do things for a reason. You may want to make some changes if you are nearing retirement and you hear your advisor say:

- "Hey, I'm an investment advisor and that's all I know."

- "Don't worry, you're long-term, you're buy-and-hold, remember."

- "It's cheaper at this price, we should dollar-cost average."

- "The market always averages 10%."

- "Look how much I made you last year."

- "Everyone lost money, it's not my fault."

- "Hey, just hang in there."

Know What, Why and How Long

One final word of caution. Find advisors who are not just concerned about their own personal wealth. Find ones who have an obvious servant heart and can care about yours. Find and work with well-rounded advisors who are experienced in a wide variety of investments, professionals who are fully schooled in tax and estate planning. The last person you should listen to is what I call a "one-trick pony" — someone who handles one product and issues warnings about other investments with which they have little or no experience. The motivation is obvious: To increase sales in their one product or service. Many, many brokers who were hypercritical of the index annuity when it was introduced are some of the same people offering them today. In conferences around the country where I have been a guest speaker, I have met hundreds of them. Finally, please remember that **experience matters**. Invest with someone who has skin — their skin — in the game. That's the PCP approach.

About the Author

Sam Foreman, founder and president of Generations Financial Group, has been serving seniors in Northwest Ohio and Southeastern Michigan for 30 years. Using his trademark PCP (primary care physician) approach, Sam brings a comprehensive and coordinated approach to investing for retirement.

The PCP approach, paired with his relentless thirst for knowledge (Sam has three degrees including a Master of Business Admiration), has earned him the rare admiration of both his clients and his peers. In 2004, Sam was chosen from among 4,000 advisors to receive the prestigious Richard M. Metcalfe Memorial Award for Faith, Persistence and Integrity. Four years later, Asset Marketing Systems named Sam "Top Mentor of the Year" (2008) for his nationally recognized success in training more than 200 financial services professionals, including stock brokers and insurance specialists.

In December 2013, William Shatner invited Sam to appear on his television special to be honored as a "Moving America Forward" entrepreneur.

Sam has been a regular contributor to Fox Toledo News and he hosts "The Financial Coach Show" on Newstalk 1370 WSPD. Thousands have heard Sam share his insights in person as he lectures widely on estate planning, retirement planning, wealth management and new investment strategies around the country. He has shared the stage and lectern with such iconic leaders as former United States President George H.W. Bush, former New York Mayor Rudy Giuliani, former U.S. Senator Bill Bradley, former U.S. Representative J.C. Watts, American politician, historian, author and political consultant Newt Gingrich, the late Walter Cronkite and many others. But his heart always remains in Maumee, Ohio.

Sam has found great joy in restoring and preserving the beautiful, historic Commercial Building on River Road in the heart of the historic district of Maumee, well known as the oldest commercial structure in Lucas County. The building was constructed in 1836 and served as a stage coach stop for travelers making their way from Detroit, Michigan, to Fort Wayne, Indiana. One of its first overnight guests was President Abraham Lincoln. In the days before the Civil War, it was used as an Underground Railway safehouse for runaway slaves. In the early days, it was also used as a post office, mercantile establishments, a restaurant and professional offices.

The building now serves as home to the offices of Sam's firm, Generations Financial Group, as well as its strategic alliances with an investment firm and a tax firm. It is also home to a banquet facility and fine dining.

"I like the synergy that we've created here. We are staying true to the original vision for this building," said Sam. "I get great satisfaction from restoring and preserving this gorgeous building so that we can bring the past forward for future generations."

Sam and his wife, Kathie, are involved in church activities locally and have been involved with several mission trips to foreign countries. Sam is known to his clients as "The Entertainer," for his ability to sing, dance, play music and impersonate famous people. His client appreciation dinners are a big event and he tries to have them often.

"We rented out 'The Pinnacle' (a large banquet hall in Maumee) for one in 2012," Sam said. "We had 780 people at that event and it was a great evening of food, fun and fellowship."

Sam and Kathie live in Maumee, which is part of the greater Toledo area. They have three married adult children: two daughters, Dawn Renee Atto and Kristi Leigh Davis, and a son, Matthew Seth-Michael Foreman, as well as seven grandchildren.

Lots of Love-
No Money
"Feel the Fear &
Do It Anyway"
-Off We Go

Marriage Vows
Sept 11, 1970

Marriage Vows
Sept 11, 1970

Acknowledgments

This is where I get to thank some people. A project like this one does not happen without the support of many people who gave selflessly of their time, wisdom and energy to bring it about.

First, I would like to thank my wife, Kathie, for her steadfastness, patience and love. I apologize for the times when I was lost in thought and my mind seemed to be off somewhere on Planet Research. I promise to make it up to you.

Next, thank you to all the other agents who work with me, and to my loyal and hardworking office staff. I could never have finished this project by the deadline without your able assistance. You never let me down.

I would also like to take the opportunity to say a sincere thank you to Pastor James Ricitelli and his wife, Ruth, for the many years of teaching and encouragement you have given me over the years. You have furthered my education in every aspect of life more than you will ever know. I will strive to emulate your example of love and selflessness.

Thanks also to my copy editor, Tom Bowen, for his counsel, insight and advice in expressing my ideas for the printed page; to Matt Newman and the Creative Department at Advisors Excel for their tireless efforts and encouragement during the production of this book.

Lastly, thank you, dear reader, for buying this book. I sincerely hope it has helped you in some way. If you have come across one idea that has improved the quality of your life, then I have succeeded.

56089927R00080

Made in the USA
Middletown, DE
19 July 2019